How to Attract Women

Laugh Your Way to
Effortless Dating & Relationship!
Attracting Women By Knowing
What They Want In A Man
(Female Psychology for
Understanding Them)

Ray Asher

Table of Contents

Your Free Resource Is Awaiting

To better help you, I've created a simple mind map you can use *right away* to easily understand, quickly recall and readily use what you'll be learning in this book.

Click Here To Get Your Free Resource

Alternatively, here's the link:

https://viebooks.club/freeresourcemind-mapforhowtoattractwomen

Introduction

Men have been asking themselves for the secret of what it takes to be attractive to women since the dawn of time. They have tried countless ways from crazy clothing and heavy colognes to pick-up lines and putting up false fronts and mindsets — an endless line of gimmicks and games to get the girl.

None of it has worked.

The reason it hasn't worked is that instead of trying to understand women and their wants and desires, men assume that they can do it on the sly with games and lies. And the majority of the time, they go down in flames.

I have spent my life learning, talking to and observing women. When I began dating, I was hopeless. I had no understanding of what women were looking for or what I could offer that would attract them. But after studying them and trial and error, I realized that there were certain rules about what they wanted and what they would respond to.

I was just like many men. Unhappy, unsuccessful with women. I didn't know how to flirt, how to talk to girls or even how to dress in a way that put my assets out there for them to see. In many cases, I tried to just be friendly and talk with women in a more laid-back manner, but this often was too subtle for them to notice I was interested.

But now I understand. **And I want to share it with you.**

I am going to show you exactly what women find attractive. Not just on the outside, but also where it really counts: on the inside. You'll learn how to have the perfect first date on into a relationship where she will stay attracted to you!

The real secret is that it's not that difficult. It's about mindset and confidence and how you view the world and opportunity. *That* is what will make you more attractive to women.

So, let's get started!

Part One: Fundamentals

Chapter 1: What Do Women Find Attractive?

Men try all sorts of things to try to be attractive to women. They try pick-up lines and clothes that they think are going to impress them. They attempt being nice, being mean and playing games. They make up stories and hooks pretending to be someone they're not.

But over and over they fail and don't understand why nothing works.

It's because you are doing what <u>you think</u> women find attractive, instead of what <u>they really</u> find attractive.

When I was younger and in college, I thought I knew what women wanted in men. I tried it all, too. The lines, the bravado, even being the Nice Guy. But nothing worked.

Then I started to pay attention and notice what worked for myself and other guys. I also paid attention to what wasn't working. I talked to women and my female friends and over time (with lots of trial and error), I discovered exactly what it was that made women attracted to men.

So, let's start with the external.

The External Is Subjective

If you think you aren't good looking, let's address that first.

External attractiveness is subjective. Everybody has a different idea of what is attractive. It's true for men and women.

Since you are a guy, let's look at it from your perspective in order to understand. Not every guy likes the same type of girl, right? Are your tastes different than your friends'?

Personally, I like tall, brunette women with curves. Doesn't mean I can't appreciate a shorter woman or blondes at all, but the first glance, total physical package that gets me going without a word is the Angelina Jolie or Megan Fox type. I love the hair, the lips, and the body. Plus, that dark smoldering look really does it for me.

Now, I have had discussions with my friends where we sat around and talked about our types. I'm sure you've done the same with your friends over a few beers. I am always surprised when I mention my type and other guys are negative and say they don't see it. They'll then offer their favorites. Blondes, redheads, short, really curvy, thin. All different types.

What I'm getting at is everybody is different and for you to think no one is going to find you attractive is just not true. There is someone for everybody. In fact, there are many someone's for everybody.

Women aren't just into the stereotypical male, tall and handsome with a six pack (though they won't necessarily turn that down, either). After talking with some of my female friends, the things that seem to interest them more is caring, funny with a sense of humor, hard worker, motivated, and easy to get along with.

You need to be secure in who you are. Until you are, you won't exude the confidence you need to attract women.

Just because you aren't a GQ model on the outside, don't despair. They will find your mindset and soul are attractive to them, and that makes up a great deal of what is going to draw a woman to you.

Don't Try to Compensate and Cover It Up

There are certain things about yourself that you just can't change, unless you are going to go in for extensive plastic surgery. You may feel that your nose is a little big, or maybe your ears are a bit small, or you don't like your eyes or a dozen other things.

We obsess over these types of things and all it does is eat away at our confidence and make us insecure.

So, some men try to compensate through external means. It might be clothing, or it might be bulking up because you are insecure about your receding hairline. We suffered through a decade of Ed Hardy shirts and gold jewelry as proof. This over-compensation is often known as peacocking.

So, don't try to add bling and accessories to "create" your personality. Women see right through this. It's different if it's organically part of who you are. **Women can tell the difference.**

Imagine two guys wearing leather motorcycle jackets. The first guy has one that is brand new, no creases and it sits on him perfectly, buttoned up, so he looks more like a fashion model than a man.

Now our second guy walks in with his weathered jacket. It's actually fitting because he has worn it, so the leather is formed to his body in places. It almost seems like an extension of him instead of a jacket.

Who do you think the woman is going to be attracted to? The weekend warrior who probably has never even touched a motorcycle or the guy who looks like he has been on some serious adventures and has stories to tell?

Yeah, exactly. I think you get my point.

On the classic television series *Married with Children*, Bud Bundy would create a new persona for school every year. In one episode, they showed him hanging up his latest costume with all the failed ones he had tried in the past. While it was done for television comedy, it's not too far from the truth.

I don't know how many suburban guys I've seen trying to pretend they were hip hop kids, guys pretending they were special forces, even dressing up in camouflage or other military-style clothing. I even remember one guy at my high school who claimed that he got into an early acceptance program (at 17!) for the Navy Seals, even though he hadn't enlisted.

The bottom line is it's not going to work. Either they are going to figure out you're full of it right then or they are going to figure it out soon thereafter. You have just created a relationship based on lies that you are going to have to keep up in order to get to know this woman.

Physical Traits Women Are Attracted To

Ok, first of all, there are a few physical traits that women find attractive, and for the most part, either you have them or you don't.

Now, don't worry about it. Think of it this way: there are certain things about women that for most men are universal. Nice lips, nice breasts, nice butt? Yeah, these are great, but not every woman has them all and by no means are you going to pass someone up because you don't have it all.

The same with women. Sure, there are certain physical attributes that women are attracted to visually, but very quickly they move past them and look for more internal things.

If you have these things, great! Accentuate them, make them more noticeable. If you don't, it's ok, we'll get to more important stuff soon.

Long Legs

A study by the Royal Society Open Science revealed that women are programmed on a primal level to look for healthy men in order to provide them with strong offspring. They do this by looking at the proportions of the body, including the length of their legs.

When hundreds of women in the study were presented with images of different body types, the thing they care about was the length of legs. Scientists theorized it was because squat body types could be a sign of diseases like diabetes or heart disease and, on a primal level, their attraction was leading them toward a healthier male. [1]

A Deep Voice

According to scientific studies, women are attracted to deep voices because they associate them subconsciously with a larger and stronger physical presence. This triggers their evolutionary need to be protected and gets them very excited. There's a reason Barry White songs do what they do.

Height and Size

Many women like a big guy whom they have to look up to. On a primal level, they feel safe and protected, and this definitely makes a man attractive. For some women, this can also mean muscle or even fat, but I would suggest the former if you have it.

You may not have the height, but at least make sure you present yourself with confidence and stand tall. Throw those shoulders back! Make sure that you are nice and tall with a strong posture. Don't puff out the chest too much, or you will appear cocky and fake.

Being in Shape

Women like lean, muscular men. There are those that are attracted to big bodybuilders, but that's a personal taste.

Most women like a lean, muscular body with a V-shape taper. Hint: Women love the lines around your waist and abs. If you can create the V that points downward, you have struck gold in this department.

Hygienic Behavior

I've touched on hygiene a few times, including in my book **How to Talk to Women**, but it is very important. A woman finds a man attractive when he takes care of himself, knows how to clean up and has pride in his appearance. You don't have to look like a male model with every hair and whisker in place, but having a sense of pride and keeping yourself presentable goes a long way when it comes to attraction.

A Great Smile

Who doesn't like a great smile? Nobody wants to hang out with someone who frowns all the time.

Make sure you keep those teeth nice and clean and white! Don't go overboard, though, with chemical bleaching; you might glow in the dark.

Forearms

Did you know that forearms are one of the sexiest things women think about a man? It's true. It shows a man's strength and power.

You can always go to the gym and build them up. Once you do, make sure you roll up your sleeves to show them off. Go easy on the weights, though. Women like lean muscles, not bulky, and very few people find those bulging veins attractive.

Men Who Look a Bit Older

Psychologists have determined that women usually prefer older men (except for cougars, but you'll have to check out *How to Flirt with Women* for more information on that subject). The reasoning is that on a primal level they see it as support, as well as the fact that men are fertile for a longer period of time, so they can be successful and still have children later in life.

Stubble

Some women really like beards, and some women really like clean-shaven men. Usually, they fall on one side of the fence or the other, but interestingly enough, almost all women like some stubble.

An Australian study showed that of four types of facial hair—clean-shaven, stubble, heavier stubble and a full beard—most women said the most attractive style was heavy stubble. Scientists determined that it gave them a feeling of maturity, masculinity, and dominance. [2]

Hint: If you go for the stubble look, get some specialty beard cream for it. It'll keep it nice and soft when she rubs it.

What Behaviors Are Women Attracted To?

As important as physical appearance is, it's also what you are like on the inside that women are interested in. So, the way you behave and interact with them is of vital importance.

Stable Behavior

Women like to know deep down that if they end up with you, you are going to take care of them or at least work with them to create an environment where you can both be safe and grow.

This means that one of the qualities she looks for is that you are stable in your handling of the world as well as finances. She wants to know how you handle things that come your way.

She likes to see that you are balanced and don't lose your temper or treat people unfairly. She wants to know you aren't unpredictable when it comes to your reaction. She wants you to be spontaneous about coming up with a fun date, but she doesn't want you to be unpredictable and throw a tantrum because your wine was opened improperly.

She also wants to know that you are stable with your finances. That you know how to save and not be frivolous on a regular basis. That you don't waste money or spend it on things you don't need.

Make It Slow

They want to see you can be calm in the moment. Women find slow, calculated and deliberate movements attractive. They perceive you as more confident and relaxed.

If you are a bigger guy, be very conscious of your movements. As a taller man myself with some muscle, I know that small moves to me can still have big consequences. Be careful.

A Sharer... to a Point

Women like a man who shares, but not too much.

They like it when you tell them a bit about your day, but they don't want to hear every detail or the inner emotions you are dealing with. If something is truly bothering you and you are in a relationship, things obviously change a bit, but we'll discuss that in Part Three of the book.

They also want you to share real experiences. A bite of their food or drink is great, as long as you don't force it and you make sure to ask if it's ok before you start. They want to have that culinary connection at that moment. It's a great way to expand on that chemistry.

Charm

There is a difference between charm and confidence. Confidence is who you are, and charm is how you show it. Charm is really about making people completely at ease when they talk with you.

Women like men who are comfortable dealing with them. Now, this isn't about being a player and knowing how to say every little thing that will get her to be yours. Charm is about being nice, knowing how to make her feel comfortable and how to just be fun to be around.

A True Sense of Humor

I'm sure you have that one friend who thinks they are a stand-up comedian. They might be funny, but when you get together, sometimes it feels like you are watching him on stage at a comedy club instead of hanging out. Suddenly it's as if all the lights are on him.

While this can be entertaining, for a bit, for the most part, it's not what women look for in a sense of humor. Women want a man who can turn a phrase in a certain way that is funny and intelligent. Maybe drop in some innuendo or teasing. They want it to feel organic and be part of the fun, not like they are sitting in the front row being told jokes by a comic.

A Positive Mindset

This is a subject I discuss at length in ***How to Talk to Women***. You need to have a positive mindset that women want to be around. It can be one of many types, but the bottom line is you have to be confident, sure of yourself and not negative.

What Do Women Not Want?

Insecurity

Women love confidence, and they hate insecurity, and it can come out in numerous ways.

- **You can't keep eye contact with her**. She is not going to make a connection with you or be attracted to you if you can't look her in the eye! She doesn't see this as cute; she sees this as emotional weakness.

- **Appearing nervous.** This means you are unsure of yourself and a woman is going to see this as a sign of a lack of confidence.

- **Actually saying that she wouldn't be into you.** This is actually putting your fear into words and handing it to her. If she had any doubts about your insecurities, they are gone now. Don't sabotage yourself!

- **Not being yourself.** If you don't express who you really are and either try to cover it up or put on a false front, she is going to see this as not being confident in who you are. Women want men who are comfortable in their own skin and with their personality.

- **Bragging.** She knows that you are trying to impress her and build yourself up. The more you do this, the more insecure she is going to realize you are.

- **Being physically tense or fidgeting.** This is a sign of nerves and a lack of confidence. It's hard to make a connection, and it's really distracting. Take a deep breath and calm down.

- **Being clingy.** Women like attention, but they don't want you to be so insecure that you feel like you have to be all over them or around them. It's a sign you don't believe that you are good enough to keep her and it will eventually drive her away.

- **Being too aggressive.** Women like men who take charge, but there is a definite difference between that and being too aggressive. You need to not push and be observant of how she reacts. Don't pressure her into a sexual conversation before she's ready or expect her to react a certain way. All this will do is make her say goodbye.

- **Being jealous.** Whether it's when you first meet her or after you've started dating, most women don't want to see you acting jealous of other men around her. It's a clear sign that you're insecure. And if you start showing it right off the bat, it's creepy.

- **Not seeing who she is.** Women want you to see who they are inside, not just the surface. When it comes to gifts, they want to know that you put thought into something. You didn't just get her flowers because that's what you do, you got her daisies because they are her favorite. They want you to understand that they also have a life, goals, and dreams and respect them for that.

Rudeness

You don't have to have the manners of a Victorian-era British lord, but you should remember things as simple as saying "please", "thank you" and "excuse me". It's also best to save any belching and farting contest with your buddies for more private venues. Even women who appreciate that sort of humor don't want to hear it in public. It'll just make them embarrassed to be around you. Also, make sure that your friends mind their manners as well. Women will judge you based on the company you keep.

Crudeness

This isn't that different from rudeness, except in this case, I'm using "crudeness" to refer to all those overtly sexually jokes and gestures that guys like to make among themselves. Honestly, these jokes and gestures aren't always appropriate among just men, let alone when women are involved. If you have any inappropriate thoughts about women, private parts, and so forth, keep them to yourself. Like with rudeness, even if a woman has that sort of humor, she might not appreciate hearing it in public, especially not when meeting you for the first time.

Insensitivity

I'm not saying that you have to cry at the drop of a hat—in fact, you really shouldn't, since women don't want oversensitivity, either. Still, don't be a cold, heartless SOB, either. If someone trips and falls close to you, show some compassion and ask if they're okay, maybe even offer to help them up. If a fight breaks out near you, don't take a side or encourage it. If possible, help de-escalate it. If a child is crying, don't act annoyed or put out. At the very least, be understanding that the parent or parents are trying their best. If you can, see if you can help out. Insensitivity and a lack of compassion are a couple of the worst traits that a woman can find in a man, along with insecurity. If they can't count on you for compassion and sympathy, they'll never be able to open up to you emotionally.

Chapter 2: The Nice Guy

Is this you? The Nice Guy?

Do you go out of your way to please a woman and give them everything they want? Do you put your own needs and desires aside to give women what they say they need, only to be put in a friend zone? Are you constantly failing with women even though you feel like you are giving them exactly what they want?

Once upon a time, women always said that they want a Nice Guy, **but do they really?**

No, they don't. They want a Good Guy, and there is a big difference.

Where Do Nice Guys Come From?

Many times, Nice Guys are created in their childhood. They may not have the same attitude in their make up as other boys, with the drive to go after what they want. Maybe they are smaller or less masculine, or that they feel they aren't as attractive as other guys.

Sometimes, it's a learned behavior stemming from their parents, often their mothers. As children, they are taught that they will get more by being "good little boys" and being pleasant and not disagreeable. They are taught that by going after what they want, they are actually being bad or causing disruption.

As they grow up, these lessons are ingrained in the boys, and they begin to use it in their dating life. If it made Mom happy it must work for women in general, right? It might work for these guys once or twice to reinforce, but most of the time, the woman will show she isn't interested in taking this relationship to the next level.

However, hope springs eternal even with Nice Guys. They are always optimistic when it comes to getting what they want.

So, after their nice actions don't get them the girl, they just think it was the wrong situation. In some cases, they might act bitter, and even wronged over the situation. They might even throw the friendship with the girl away, acting as if it doesn't matter to them. This isn't the right way to go about things. Sometimes, it just won't work out with a girl, this doesn't mean you throw everything away. Maybe next time it'll work better for them. And they try again, and again and the vicious circle keeps going.

Being a Nice Guy Is Actually Toxic

If you are a nice guy who has problems dating women, you are probably very confused. You feel like you are doing everything right, but in reality, you have absolutely no success. And when you do meet a woman and go out a few times, it ends before anything gets serious. Why?

Because Nice Guys are Actually Very Selfish!

A Nice Guy is acting upon personal reasons that are often hidden from the women he interacts with. These reasons can become very toxic. Nice Guys have inner turmoil going all the time.

- They feel slighted because they give and give and don't receive a return on their "nice investment."

- They fix other people's problems and can become upset when it isn't reciprocated even though the other person has no idea they wanted that.

- They are constantly seeking approval from others instead of being self-secure.

- They have a drive to do things the right way in order to gain approval, instead of self-worth.

- They repress their feelings because they don't want to upset people and lose their Nice Guy status.

- They can't make their needs a priority, which leads to a lack of self-reliance.

- They are actually being dishonest and disingenuous because they hide their feelings and mistakes and say what they think people want to hear versus the truth.

- They can be very passive aggressive and actually hold in rage until it explodes, damaging relationships.

"Secure Your Own Mask First"

Have you ever been on an airplane and they go through the safety drill before takeoff? And when they get to those masks, what do they always say?

"Secure your own mask first and then assist the other person."

It's the same with dating. If you aren't secure and happy and getting what you need, how can you do the same for her? You need to look and see what someone offers you.

It sounds shallow, <u>but it's not</u>. Why would you want to be in a relationship with a woman where you aren't getting what you need from her? It doesn't matter if it's sex, communication or just emotional support. You need to create the mindset so that you understand you have needs and if you are with her, you need to have them fulfilled.

Now, I'm not saying you should break up with her if she won't rub your feet every night. But you deserve basic happiness, respect, and fulfillment from the start.

A Nice Guy won't think that way. He'll put that mask on everybody else on the plane before his own and not understand why he's feeling light-headed. He'll then get angry because he took care of others and they didn't take care of him.

The Mindset of the Nice Guy

On the outside, the Nice Guy seems... well, nice! But inside, there is actually a lot going on, and most of it isn't very pleasant. Inside his brain, it's a maelstrom of fear, anger, and passive aggressiveness.

- They think if they are nice to everyone, everyone will love them.

- "If I meet other people's needs without them having to ask for it, they will reciprocate and do the same for me."

- "If I do everything in a happy, nice way, everything will work out for me."

- They will do almost anything for others, leaving their own life a wreck.

- They let other people walk all over them because they don't want to be accused of being a troublemaker.

- They will never say "No," no matter how much it might be an imposition.

- They seek the approval of other people for their self-worth.

- They put other people's wants and needs before their own.

- Nice Guys tend to downplay their masculine nature in order to try to get closer to people.

The problem is that by doing this, you are giving your power away to other people and "unseen" forces like fate.

And what happens when things don't work out? You are left holding the bag and feeling powerless, but you created things in such a way that you needed to interact with people for your happiness, and they won't want to be around you.

What Do Women Think of Nice Guys?

We also need to look at how women view these nice guys. Many "nice guys" are notorious for thinking that women owe them something (and that something is usually sex), just for being friends with her. They have no interest in just being friends with that girl. One thing to realize among female circles is that nice guys are viewed with the idea "if he says he's a nice guy, he isn't."

Not that long ago, some of my friends and I went out for a couple drinks after work. There was a good mix of men and women, so the discussions were getting very spirited at times. At some point, the conversation turned to dating and relationships. One of my male buddies who had seemed unlucky in that area asked our female friends, "I've been hanging out with this one girl forever. I drop everything for her, listen to her problems, help her run errands whenever she asks, but all she does is friend zone me. And now she's seeing some suit! What the heck? Why wouldn't she want to go out with me? I'm a nice guy!"

Some of our male friends agreed with him, but I cringed hard. The women? If looks could kill, there'd have been charges for five counts of murder that night. Fortunately, one of the more level-headed of our female friends calmly told him, "Frank, we love you, but you need to get over yourself. If you really care about this woman, you should be glad to be her friend. Isn't being her friend better than nothing at all? And what about us? Are you mad about being in the 'friend zone' with us? And newsflash, just because you've been nice with her does not mean that she owes you shit. You're the reason why women can't say that we want a nice guy anymore. You say you're a nice guy, but you aren't."

That was a huge slap in the face for all the men there. Even though I already knew not to say something like that, her words still affected me deeply. Why was my friend belittling his friendship with a woman just because he wanted to sleep with her? Since that night, he has not complained once about being put in the "friend zone" or about being a "nice guy", and as far as I can tell, he's still friends with that woman. Only time will tell if he stays a reformed nice guy.

More and more women are realizing the truth about self-proclaimed "nice guys", and they aren't liking it. The term is quickly becoming as dreaded as the phrase "friend zone", if not more so.

What Is the Good Guy?

Now I am going to lay some of the blame for this situation right at the feet of women. How often have you heard a woman say something like "If only I could meet a Nice Guy!" and then they date the Nice Guy and are completely unhappy? Then what do they say again? "Why can't I just meet a Nice Guy..."

The problem is they are confusing Nice Guy with the Good Guy, which is actually what they want. What women really want is a good guy, someone who treats them right, someone who will be there to comfort them, to help them, to be by their side.

Over the years, nice guy has changed its meaning. It used to be what we think of as nice guy. But now, it is more of someone who pretends to be nice but who thinks women owe them something. Men were the ones who started changing the term, and for women, getting the two mixed up could be a big reason why they aren't finding the kind of guy they actually want. Fortunately, women are starting to realize what nice guys now are, so perhaps soon they'll learn what a good guy is.

A Good Guy is two things. First, he is a man who treats a woman with respect, honesty and passion. Second, he is a good fit for a woman because he has the masculine qualities that are going to fulfill them and make a woman happy.

A Good Guy has his stuff together and is confident and self-reliant. He has a positive mindset and a balanced life. He is accountable and genuine, which is what women are really looking for.

So How Is a Good Guy Different?

- He treats a woman with respect and has open communication. He doesn't expect her to read his mind and doesn't do things expecting reciprocation or some silent contract that fulfills him internally.

- He is thoughtful, but not overbearing or stifling. He knows how to give a woman the space she needs but also when to be there for her.

- He doesn't cheat or play manipulative games. He's mature and treats her the same.

- He lets his woman know she is desired and wanted but doesn't suffocate her.

- He isn't cruel, even when they are fighting. He knows how to have an intelligent argument that leads to fixing things, not just trying to hurt each other.

- He makes a woman feel secure and protected. This isn't just about physical protection but giving a woman support so she can be the person she wants to be.

- He makes plans but doesn't boss her around. He is decisive but takes the woman's interests and feelings into consideration.

- He does things because he wants women to be happy and with him, not because he is trying to get something out of you.

- He sees potential and isn't just looking for notches on his bedpost. He isn't trying to use his Good Guy status just to get a woman into bed. This relationship might not be forever, but he's not looking around for other options while he's with a woman.

- Doesn't devalue the friendship he has with the woman. He knows this is important, not just a way to get something from the woman (like sex).

How Can I Change My Nice Guy Habits?

The good news is you can break this cycle.

- First and foremost, realize that your **happiness needs to come from within**. You cannot rely on the actions of others to fulfill you. Bedding a thousand girls will not fulfill you, or money or a host of other things. You need to understand that. Remember, the woman does not owe you anything just for being your friend. Just because you are nice to her, doesn't mean she has to sleep with you. Becoming her friend might just end up being the best thing to happen to you and might become one of the most meaningful relationships in your life, even if it doesn't go where you originally planned.

- **Learn to say "No."** You need to set boundaries and understand that you can't (and shouldn't) be all things to all people.

- **Take care of your own needs first.** This doesn't mean being selfish, but as I said above, you have to put your own mask on before you can help others.

- **Take responsibility**. Understand that by placing unspoken demands on others, you are actually being toxic, unfair and petty.

- **Be concise in conversation.** Ask small, to-the-point questions. You aren't trying to please people with flattery or talking a lot when getting information. Be direct and to the point, though pleasant.

- **Don't seek external approval.** You need to find your approval within. You cannot base your value on what others (especially women) think of you.

- **Have goals and don't ignore them in order to help others.** Be nice and supportive and help when you can, but you need to achieve your own dreams and goals.

- **Don't avoid confrontation.** When you don't address issues, they simmer and fester inside. That's how passive aggression begins, and then it all erupts. Tackle issues before they get too big and do it in a constructive way and as politely as possible. However, don't be a pushover and know that you have the right to be happy.

Agreement Should Not Be Your Go-To Move

Too often, Nice Guys don't want to cause problems when they talk to women, so they agree with everything they say. The hope is that this will endear them to the woman because you make a connection through agreement.

Be yourself. If you disagree with a comment or statement, say so. Be nice, don't be argumentative, but speak your mind. She's going to value that more than blindly agreeing with her.

Balance

Sometimes Nice Guys spend so much time trying to please women (and others) that they lose sight of the balance in their life. They don't make time for their guy friends or even their alone time. By balancing your life, you will understand how you need different interactions to be happy and fulfilled.

You Are Not Missing an Opportunity

One of the main thoughts behind the behavior of a Nice Guy is that if he's always there for a woman, eventually she'll turn and look at him with different eyes. Instead of seeing a friend, she'll realize that she loves this man and fall into his arms. Then the music plays, and you realize that your life really is a romantic move. Fade to black as you kiss...

Oh, stop. Life isn't a movie.

You aren't going to miss out on some magic moment where she suddenly realizes that you are the one she loves. By dropping everything and rushing to her side, you are not making yourself indispensable.

In fact, if she were going to suddenly have a realization, **it's because you were not there.** It's more likely that she misses you and realizes she is interested when you are not there. Remember, absence makes the heart grow fonder.

Get Rid of The One for One Mindset

Nice Guys tend to keep track. They create this mindset where they are waiting for things to come back to them. They did a certain number of nice things for a woman, so it's time for her to reciprocate.

Except the world doesn't work that way. You need to just be yourself. Be a good guy and do thoughtful things and pay compliments, but don't do it expecting a one-for-one return on your investment. Just do it because that's who you are.

Increase Your Independence

Independence is something that women are always attracted to. They love that you can be alone and get your stuff done.

So, add to this. The more independent you can be, the more confidence you will build. Believe me, they will notice this. Instead of allowing your life to fall to pieces because you are helping others, you'll be making your own life stronger, which women will respond to.

Create Your Own Schedule

Have you ever been getting ready to do something fun or maybe even work and you get that text or call that someone wants your time for something that's really not that important?

Do you say you can't because you're wrapped up in something or do you drop it all, putting your own life on hold to go off and attend to someone else's needs?

We know what the Nice Guy does.

Your time and schedule are not only important, but they are also valuable. Give it to people who deserve it but also guard it. You need to take care of your responsibilities and needs first.

So, who do you want to be? The Nice Guy or the Good Guy?

Chapter 3: The Masculine Mindset and What It Means to Be a Man

There was a time when being a man meant a few things: take care of your family, stand up for yourself, be honest. Some people would say drinking, fighting and swearing. And, of course, getting the girl.

That was it. Generations grew up with the concept that if you acted like John Wayne or James Bond, you were a man. Everything else be damned, as long as people looked up to you, you were a man.

But as society has evolved and our view of the world has changed, it's become a bit more complicated.

To me, being a man is more than just bringing home the bacon and being able to take care of yourself in a bar fight. It's deeper than that. It's about values and responsibility. It's not about age, but it is about experience.

What Does it Mean to Be a Man

Responsibility

A man takes responsibility for himself and his actions. If he does something wrong, he makes amends and fixes what he did. He keeps his promises. If he has children, he cares for them and raises them properly.

Partnership

There was a time when a man was expected to take on all responsibility himself. The woman stayed home and would never work. He would bring home a paycheck and work two jobs if he had to.

The woman wasn't expected to be involved in matters of work or finance, just to keep the home clean and comfortable. As Michael Corleone said, "Never ask me about my business."

Has that ever changed in modern times? With most families requiring both people to work just to survive, the changes in women's rights and pay and a shifting of our society to a more balanced playing field in gender roles, a man needs to look at the world differently.

I believe that today's man needs to have the skills to have an equal partnership. It's up to the two of you to come to an understanding of what your roles are, but that partnership and communication are vital. A man can't just make a blanket statement that he'll take care of everything. He has to work with his partner. But that doesn't mean you have to become weak or dependent. You can do more by sharing responsibilities as a team.

Maybe Take a Break

Here's a suggestion that might work, or it might not. It really depends on how radically you might be changing your life and the way you approach yourself and women.

Consider taking a bit of a vacation.

Remember when you were in school and classes would end for the summer and kids would come back after the break and have a different attitude, different clothes, maybe even have grown a few inches or muscled up?

You might want to consider this. Consider taking a little mini vacation from women, friends, and social life. Not too long, maybe a few weeks.

This will give you a chance to make some changes, tweak some things about how you approach life and dating. Spend some time with yourself thinking things out, figuring out what your goals are with life and with women.

That way, when you start to see people you know, any changes you implement won't seem drastic, like you are trying something new. That way, they will comment on how you've changed since the last time they saw you and they like the changes. Or even better, new women won't see the process; they'll only see (and be attracted to) the result.

Masculine Behaviors

No matter what, there are certain behaviors that are definitely masculine, and burping and farting at the dinner table are not among them.

Confidence

It is very masculine to be confident. It is the top thing that women respond to. A confident man has self-worth and independence. He is self-reliant and doesn't need to go to others for fulfillment or validation.

I cannot stress enough how important confidence is. I have mentioned it time and again in this book and my others. In order to be successful with the opposite sex, you **MUST** find your confidence.

Assertiveness

A masculine man knows what he wants and goes for it. This is different than the Alpha Male, which is basically just a name for a boorish guy. It's not just about feeling a sense that something should be yours because you deserve it; it's about how to figure out how to achieve your goals. It comes down to getting stuff down, and that is very masculine.

Dominance

There is a difference between being dominant and being a bully or cruel. Dominant is standing up for yourself and what is yours. Sometimes it's not about words but simply body language and the vibe you give off.

I mentioned in my other books I am very tall, so I automatically give off a dominant vibe. I can come across as a bit intense because of my size, so that helps as well.

Courage

Courage doesn't have to be about going to war or saving someone from a burning building. Sometimes courage is simply about getting up in the morning or being able to take a chance in order to get what you want. Often, it's about standing up for what you believe and not changing in the face of pressure from others.

Women value courage, even in smaller situations. When you get up and take a chance talking to a girl, that takes courage and women notice that.

Masculine Polarity

Ever heard the term opposites attract? Sometimes it's not quite true. If you are with someone who is too different than you, you won't have any commonalities, and you won't be able to find a deeper connection or relationship.

However, when it comes to male and females, you absolutely want the opposite attraction.

Masculine polarity is the idea that the more masculine you are and the more feminine she is, the more attracted you will be to each other. And it works.

If you are too much alike in your masculinity/femininity poles, you won't be as attracted to each other as you could be. The more you amplify your masculine traits, the more her feminine traits will be attracted to you. It's actually really simple.

But you need to make sure they are the correct traits, like we have been discussing. If your traits like confidence, decisiveness, and courage stand strong, her feminine traits will respond to you.

Be a Man of Purpose

We all ask ourselves those existential questions. Why am I here? What is the meaning of life? What is my purpose?

For generations going back to the cavemen, a man's purpose was simple. Survive, protect and procreate.

That was it! For the duration of their short adult lives, they hunted, fed their family and tried not to get trampled by mastodons. Life was pretty simple.

But over time, that purpose has changed. Suddenly, it wasn't life-threatening to get food. Life expectancy went from being lucky to see your 30s to averaging almost a hundred years.

As that happened, a man's purpose became less defined. We used to have rites of passage and those disappeared. Now men wander around try-ing to figure out how to be men.

Now, it's not a bad thing. The world we live in is safer, more rewarding and honestly more fun. I would much rather be able to go to a movie than sit and stare at cave paintings.

Also, there is a great equality of the sexes that makes life more enjoyable. Men have become more understanding and tolerant and have grown to understand the missteps that have led to do-mestic violence and abuse.

But it comes back to that question... what is a man's purpose?

Yearning for Adventure and Risk

In the old days, a man's life had the risk and the ability to prove themselves. In tribal cultures, they were given a task or quest to fulfill in order to achieve manhood. Even in our own culture for many years a man's rite of passage was serving in the military or being drafted.

Now men have to find ways to challenge them-selves and prove their manliness. Unfortunately, a lot of our male youth have to do this through fan-tasy. Playing video games or participating in sports.

Why Is That Important?

So, let me ask you a question. Do you listen to your gut feelings?

There was a time when men were trained to be able to react to fear. It was part of their life, so they honed their instinct to know what to do. And since it was something they experienced regularly whether in war, hunting or just the rough and tumble times they lived in, they developed instinct.

However, in modern society, our instinct is dulled. When people get scared or are in a dangerous situation, they think they will respond bravely, but in reality, they freeze.

I don't blame them. You are suddenly faced with a situation that you have no experience in.

I had a female friend who trained in martial arts and was not the type of woman to be afraid. She felt very secure in her skills. One day, she was waiting for a bus when a homeless woman (who was later medically evaluated as having mental issues) walked up to her and cold cocked her, right across the face. No warning, nothing. Just bam!

My friend froze. She didn't know what to do. Even with all her martial arts training, she had never had any practical experience. So, the woman hit her again.

Luckily, several bystanders separated the homeless woman and authorities quickly arrived and took the woman somewhere to get the mental help she needed, but my friend was devastated. She had not used any of her knowledge. She had just frozen. Why?

She had no practical real-world experience. She knew how to deal with a guy grabbing her from behind, she knew how to strike an opponent who comes right up at her, she had all this knowledge but no experience in real-world situations.

Should she have struck back? Probably not, the woman who hit her didn't know what she was doing. But my friend could have defended herself at least, blocking the second attack. But she didn't.

It's like men. We have lost the real-world experience. We tend not to take chances or learn to trust our male instincts because we have no experience in how to do it.

We have to learn to take chances and listen to our guts. It's the same with women, too. You need practical experience of talking and flirting with them in order to get your instincts working properly.

How to Improve Yourself

So, you're perfect, right? Don't you need any self-improvement?

Here's some honest truth. Everyone can improve themselves. I try to do it every day.

This is different from gaining new skills (although we will be discussing that later in the book.) This is about taking an honest look at your personality, mindset and characteristics and being honest about what you see.

This is about looking at yourself and putting in the work to be a better man and a better human being. Make changes to your life and mindset and try to be a better human being every day.

Surround Yourself with the Right Men

Associate with men you respect and who you would be proud to be associated with. Don't listen to negative, cruel or hateful guys. Get rid of friendships with men who are bad influences or tend to bring you down.

Plus, when you bring a woman around, you want to her to be able to trust your friends. She will respect you more for choosing whom you hang out with wisely.

...And Women

I sing the praises of having female friends in all my books. They can really help you when it comes to learning what women like, and the right ones will help you become a compassionate, well-rounded person. Like with your male friends, get rid of any of the negative and hateful female influences in your life and focus on the ones the build you up.

Having female friends might become a bit of a problem if you find a woman who turns out to be the jealous type. However, if she really is right for you, she will learn how to cope with it and not let her problems ruin your relationships. If not, you might want to reevaluate your relationship with her.

Health and Exercise

Physical health has come into play in many of the subjects in this book, and it's because it really is in every part of your life.

Being healthy means you are not only aware of yourself, but by improving your health, you have a more active quality of life. You can be more effective, do more and generally be a better person. If you feel sick or overweight, it comes out through your actions and interactions.

Education

We will get more into this later, but it is vital that you understand the world around you and how things work and are always looking for new knowledge. You should be hungry for it because that is how you improve yourself.

Goals

You can't change if you don't know where you are going. So, it is vital to set goals and milestones, whether it is physical, mental or emotional.

There's nothing wrong with rewarding reaching your goals, either. It's actually a great thing to do. You put in the hard work, you deserve it.

Forget the Past

You can't improve and move forward if you are chained to the past. Yes, we do learn from our mistakes, but if you stay tethered to them, carry-ing guilt or negative feelings, you can't move for-ward and risk becoming a victim.

Look to the Future, but Don't Be Enslaved by It

Like I said, you need to set goals and milestones and strive towards them. At the same time, you can't keep your eyes so focused on the future that you forget to live in the present. You don't want to spend so much time living only for a single goal only to reach, look back and wonder where all the fun times with friends and family went. The joy is in the journey.

Abundance Mindset

Do you ever walk outside hoping that you'll meet a woman but when you look around you don't see any? Or you think none of these women will be in-terested in you?

You can't do that. **You need to have a mental-ity of abundance.**

This is a positive attitude that you believe that you have abundant options when it comes to women. That when you look around not only do you notice women, but you know that you can talk to them and date them. You need to really understand and believe that they want to talk to you.

But the key to abundance is that that the more prepared you are, the more chances you'll get. You have to hone some of your skills in order to truly use it to your advantage.

Observe and Absorb

You need to learn as much as you can about how women think, what they want and how they interact with men. I would like to think that in this book and *How to Flirt with Women* and *How to Talk to Women* I've given you a pretty good roadmap, but nothing beats real life experience.

Always be paying attention. Listen when you are sitting at restaurants or just waiting for the bus. Pay attention to what women say to men or other women. Listen to how they talk about their men and what makes them happy or upset. How do they talk about their needs from their men? Are they being satisfied? What are they missing?

Practice

If you wanted to play in the major leagues, would you just show up for a tryout or would you spend years practicing until you were big league material?

Of course, you would practice. That's how you get better.

It's the same with abundance. Practicing conversational skills and working on your ability to flirt and chat with them is how you get better.

Of course, working on women you are interested in is the biggest help, but don't stop there. Talk to all sorts of women. Flirt with the woman behind the counter, learn to use your smile with strangers.

Aim High

Don't ever think that a woman is out of your league or that you don't have a chance. By being ambitious, not only do you have more women to choose from you also push yourself. It's like when you play tennis; you get better by playing with better opponents.

The same can be said with meeting and dating women. By being ambitious and trying all sorts of different women who you incorrectly think you don't have a chance with, you are going to hone your skills and also up your confidence.

Extend Your Social Circle

It's vital to always be creating new social contacts and widening your circle of friends and acquaintances.

This serves a number of purposes in your life, more than just your interaction with women. It will allow you to create business contacts, which will help you get jobs and succeed in your career. Plus, if you surround yourself with positive and hardworking influences, you will have a support structure and not be dragged down by negativity.

It's always better, though, to have a small group of high-quality friends than a larger group of acquaintances that don't have as much of a positive effect on your life.

Through this social circle, you will be able to meet new people, become more socially strong and interactive. Your confidence will go up, and you will indeed be more successful in your life.

Sometimes it is time to leave some friends and acquaintances behind. If they are not positive influences or you don't enjoy being around them, it's fine to begin to remove them from your life.

When it comes to women, your social circle is an amazing tool to meet them. By going out with friends, you get put in situations where you will meet more people and women.

Also, you never know who is a friend of a friend that you might get introduced to.

Why to Not Put Women on a Pedestal

When I was dating in my 20s, I had a bad habit of assuming that the women I was going out with knew what they were saying.

You see, I like intelligent women so, as I would get to know them, I assumed that they knew what they were talking about and if it was a subject I didn't know, I would give them the benefit of the doubt and assume they were correct.

I was putting them on an intellectual pedestal. Many guys do the same thing, whether it's for beauty, sex appeal or just because they care about them.

This is going to lead to some problems with both of you. I remember one time when a woman I was dating would try to get my opinion on something she was doing at work. It wasn't a topic I knew much about, and so I deferred to the classic "what do you think is best?"

In this situation, I assumed that she knew more what she was talking about and would be able to make the best decision. I had no idea about the topic and honestly wasn't putting much effort into learning about it.

Later, I realized that she had been trying to share a part of her life with me. She wanted my opinion and my input, and if I hadn't been so busy putting her on a pedestal of being so intelligent and knowing better, I could have given her some of the support she needed. Sure, I might not know much about the topic, but by being present and at least showing my support, I could have given her more of what she needed.

The problem is that when you do this, you are creating an ideal and no one is going to live up to that. In the end, both of you are going to get hurt, and the relationship isn't going to end well.

This causes you to ignore the negatives and be drawn into the zone of Nice Guy. Then, because you don't want to think that you've been wrong, you'll double down and think she's perfect and dive deeper into your relationship.

Plus, women won't respond to this in the long run. They'll either get bored with you or maybe even start to take advantage of you.

Chapter 4: The Renaissance Man

There was a time when men were looked up to if they had a number of skills. They would learn multiple languages, have talents in a variety of trades and be versed in politics, philosophy, and business. We called them Renaissance Men.

One perfect example was U.S. President Thomas Jefferson. Besides being a founding father and helping draft the Declaration of Independence, he was an architect, author, farmer and interested in dozens of other subjects on which he wrote numerous publications.

Sometimes we call these people "polymaths", but all it means is someone who is good at many different things.

In modern society, people tend to stay in their comfort zones, only learning skills or information that is pertinent to their career or narrow field of interests.

And women hate that.

Women like men who are adventurous, who know about things. It's not only to your benefit in the pursuit of women but as a human being. By being more well-rounded and knowing other topics, you can be more successful in work, romance and life in general. **You'll have an interesting life, and any woman will want to be part of it.**

It makes you more interesting. You may have seen the famous beer campaign with the most Interesting Man in the World. Why was he interesting and appealing to women? It wasn't the beer he drank; it was the life he led. He had a variety of skills and did interesting things. To women, that is fascinating and sexy.

I think author Robert Heinlein said it best:

"A human being should be able to change a diaper, plan an invasion, butcher a hog, conn a ship,

design a building, write a sonnet, balance accounts, build a wall, set a bone, comfort the dying, take orders, give orders, cooperate, act alone, solve equations, analyze a new problem, pitch manure, program a computer, cook a tasty meal, fight efficiently, die gallantly. Specialization is for insects."

Music

I went to a very rural high school, so rural that it could take an hour to get to the nearest Walmart. Yeah, it was that rural.

My junior year of high school a new student arrived who had just moved from a major city. He dressed different and listened to strange new music. We had never heard some of these songs before, let alone the bands. Many of the other students began to make fun of him, tease him about his music with derogatory and honestly pretty juvenile insults.

Flash forward to my senior year. Suddenly, the music that this new student had been listening to was at the top of the charts. Everyone was into it and even dressing a bit different, more like the new student.

Music tastes are different and cyclical. The more you open yourself up to different styles, the more there is to enjoy. If you like a certain musician or song, there's nothing wrong with that. Personally? I like pop music, but I also enjoy jazz and some country music.

By opening yourself up to more music, you'll seem more worldly and educated. You never want to ask what her favorite band is and be stumped because you've never heard of them. And even worse, never ask, let her answer and then start to be negative about her choices. That's a quick way to shut down any conversation.

Music is personal, and by insulting her choices, you are driving her away. You don't have to fake it, but her uniqueness is what you are attracted to.

Current Events

I mentioned before that I am a news junkie. I understand that it's not for everyone, but you at least need to know what's going on in the world.

Part of being a responsible man is being aware of your surroundings, and this includes the news. You don't have to digest every little bit or spend the entire day watching cable news, but be aware, especially of major events. And make sure you know what you are talking about! You don't ever want to dive into a conversation and suddenly realize you don't know what you are saying.

Plus, it's a pretty nice way to impress a woman. You won't always be just talking to her, but there will be other people around. Imagine how it will feel if someone says something about current events and you are able to reply, knowing exactly what is going on.

Cooking

I am a horrible cook. It's just not one of my skills. However, I have three dishes that I can cook very well. I have one for breakfast, lunch, and dinner.

You don't need to take culinary classes (although it's a great way to meet women, as we have discussed in **How to Talk to Women**), but you should have a handful of dishes that you know how to cook without using a microwave. You need one that you can make for a romantic dinner, one you can whip together for lunch and, of course, a breakfast that you can make when the two of you wake up.

Who knows, maybe you'll find you enjoy cooking. That's a skill that women absolutely love in a man.

Besides loving to be pampered with a home-cooked meal, women also appreciate not having to shoulder this responsibility alone in a relationship, whether she still thinks that a woman's place is "in the kitchen" or not.

Physical Fitness

There is a difference between simply going to the gym and understanding physical fitness.

A lot of guys go to the gym a few times a week, do their exercises and go home. That's it. They don't give fitness one more thought until they go to the gym again.

Eventually, they'll stop going because they figure they don't really need it or because they don't see any real results. Eventually, they'll start to gain weight, have health problems, and they (and their woman) start to ask, "What happened?"

The man who understands physical fitness and how to properly stay healthy has an entirely different approach. They understand how to exercise and when. They know about recovery, proper nutrition and how muscles really work and grow. They know which exercises to do and what results they will get. They understand that it's a process and they need to put the work in before they see results.

Bartender

Learn a couple of classic cocktails that you can mix. Also, learn the proper way to pour a beer. Impress her by learning her favorite drink.

These are all extremely simple things to learn but will make you a hero in her eyes. And don't stop there. Make sure you have other skills under your belt.

- Learn to change a tire.

- Learn to change the oil in the car.

- Make sure you know how to start a fire, put up a tent and other camping type activities.

- Know how to put out a grease fire. While it's simple to learn, it's different from putting out a regular fire and a surprising number of people don't know how to do it. Learn this, and you'll become her in-kitchen fireman.

- Drive. It sounds simple, but when she's in the car with you, she wants to feel safe and secure in your skills. Make sure you know how to drive defensively and safely. Also, learn how to parallel park.

- Drive a stick shift! Learn how to drive a manual car. It's just a skill that helps because you never know when you may end up behind the wheel of a car. It could be as a designated driver or due to an accident or injury. And there is something manly about driving a stick shift that women really dig. Plus, all the openings for sexual innuendo!

- Know how to jumpstart a car.

- Basic first aid. If you come to her rescue when she's hurt, even if it's just a tiny paper cut, you'll be her hero. Plus learn CPR and the Heimlich Maneuver.

- Sew/fix your clothes. You don't need to learn major sewing skills, but the ability to sew on a button or fix small things shows her that not only are you independent you'll do what you must to get jobs done.

- Unclog a drain/toilet. Let's face it, accidents happen. It doesn't matter how they happen, but if you're able to unclog the blocked drain or toilet, she'll be incredibly grateful.

- Know how to make simple repairs around the house. You don't have to be Tim Taylor but know how to fix a squeaky door or a leaky faucet. She might already know how to do this herself, but she'll probably appreciate an extra set of helping hands.

- Use a map - Sure, everything is GPS these days, but what happens if you don't have a signal? You need to learn how to use a map, follow direction directions, use a map scale and operate a compass.

- Learn to give a proper massage. When I say proper, I mean one that feels good, actually works out stress and isn't just a precursor for hands-on action.

- Throw a punch- You don't want to get into any fights, and it's about the mechanics more than hurting anyone. Many women don't know how to throw a proper punch. It might even come up in conversation. However, if you can, learn how to de-escalate a situation before it gets to this point.

- Learn to be a mediator. While women can appreciate a man who throws a good punch, they'll appreciate someone strong enough to de-escalate a situation with his words alone more.

In fact, things that men can do that women traditionally have a difficult time at are common conversation topics. I dated a girl once who was fascinated with how men can spit because she couldn't do it. You never know what their interest might be.

Cleaning

In this book and in *How to Flirt with Women* and *How to Talk to Women*, I discussed personal hygiene and dressing yourself, but you also need to know how to keep your own home clean. Know how to properly clean the shower and bathroom.

Make sure to properly vacuum and sweep and clean the kitchen. Know how to wash the dishes by hand in case there is no dishwasher. Not only do you want her to feel comfortable in your home, but you also want her to know you value it by keeping it clean and organized.

Knowing how to do your own laundry is also a big plus. If she's going to be with you, she wants to be your partner, not your mother.

Social and Community Responsibility

A true Renaissance Man understands the importance of giving back to his community and society, whether through volunteering or organizations and charity or other groups that help the community like Rotary or fraternal organizations.

This shows that the man understands the values of others and helping them. Women respond to this very strongly.

Like I discuss in ***How to Flirt with Women***, volunteering is also a great way to meet women. Volunteering to work with senior citizens and children and at pet adoption events can also show off your compassionate side. Women love that.

Appreciating the Arts

You don't have to be a great artist, but a Renaissance Man understands art and its importance. If he doesn't like something, he doesn't try to devalue it verbally or make fun of those who do like it. He understands that by broadening his horizons, he can understand people better.

Travel

The more you see of the world, the more you understand the world and yourself.

Open yourself up to travel. I know it can be expensive, but it doesn't have to be around the world. Consider road trips or just exploring your own city. The more you learn, the more educated and interesting you become.

Focus

There is a danger of spreading yourself thin when it comes to activities and goals. You need to be careful to not lose focus on your goals or become what some people might label as "all over the place."

Make sure you finish what you start and don' take on other tasks or responsibilities if they're going to weigh you down. You don't want to start being known as someone who doesn't finish what they start or follow through when you gave your word.

Jack of All Trades, Master of None

You don't have to be an expert in everything you do, but you do need to give it your all and work to learn a certain basic mastery. If you fail and discover it's not one of your skills, that's fine.

However, never lie to a woman. If you rode a horse once, don't tell her you used to be a cowboy. You might have taken a few martial arts classes but don't try to convince her you're a trained killer.

When you try to pass yourself off as an expert in something you are not, all you are doing is putting off insecurity vibes. When you are secure in yourself and your skills, you want to share your stories not brag about skills. There is a difference.

When you fake brag, it's obvious. "I did this; I did that. Once when I was in such and such amazing place..."

We all want to make ourselves look a little better. We want to put our best foot forward, and we assume that by bragging and saying we are the expert, even in things we know nothing about, that we will be able to impress those around us.

This can, and usually will, backfire against us. At some point, someone will actually be an expert in the field that you are trying to show off in, and they will bury you in the ground. This will make you lose trust with others, can make you look like a fool, and hurts your reputation more than anything else.

I remember one time when I was talking to a woman I liked while waiting for our food. I decided I really wanted to impress her and started to brag a bit about my knowledge of fine wine or something similar and how I knew all the local winery owners around.

This was going great, and she seemed really impressed. That is, until a friend of hers showed up, one who was actually the daughter of one of the wine owners I pretended to know. It took two seconds for her to know my story was a lie, and it instantly lost me any respect with the woman I was interested in.

The good news here is that you have a lot of really unique skills and interests, and there is bound to be one (that is true) that you can share with the woman. Why not focus on those and actually maintain your chances?

Fun Skills

Not everything you do has to be serious. Learn some fun little skills. Many of these only take a short amount of time to learn and can always be great to throw into a conversation or to break the ice or tension. If you already have a unique skill or talent, use that as a way to start a conversation and break the ice.

Opening a Bottle without a Bottle Opener

No, not with your teeth. Learn different ways to pop that cap. Using a countertop, a key, or even a dollar bill.

If you fold a dollar bill into a small square, it will be strong enough to pop the cap. Try it!

If you want a real skill, though you might not have much of a chance to demonstrate, learn the art of opening a champagne bottle with a sabre. But I would highly suggest being very careful where you demonstrate this skill.

Play Cards

Know the basics of card games and how to play. You don't have to be a professional gambler, but learn the hands and basic rules of poker, black-jack, craps, and roulette.

Also, learn how to properly shuffle cards and with some style!

Pool

Learn the basics of pool and how to make certain simple shots. You don't have to become a shark, but you need to learn to be good enough to win and to teach a woman how to play if she doesn't already know.

A little warning: A lot of women know how to play pool, but they will pretend that they don't in order to see if you really do. Sometimes, they just enjoy being shown and want to watch you lean over the table or have you lean over with them to show them how to make a shot.

Learn How to Make a Good $%#&!! Cup of Coffee

I am not a coffee snob, I will admit. I like it black and strong. But I realize I am in the minority, especially when it comes to women, though I can appreciate a well-made, good blend of coffee.

So, learn how to make an amazing cup of coffee with the right amount of cream and sugar if desired.

Magic

Learn a couple of magic tricks but don't use them on a woman, save them for kids and she'll be impressed by how you entertained the little ones.

Cup Stacking

This might sound boring, but it's actually pretty cool. Just look up "cup stacking" on YouTube and you'll find all these videos of people quickly stacking and unstacking cups, making different sizes of pyramids, flipping the cups, and all sorts of tricks. The best part is that since the initial wave of the craze was a few years ago, people have mostly gotten past it by now, and so cup stacking is once again a novel talent.

Bar Bets

Every guy should have a few bars tricks up his sleeve. Make sure you practice these a few times before trying them out in public.

- Tell someone you can tell which side the match heads are in without opening or shaking a box of matches. When they agree, try to balance it evenly on a knife and the side that is heavier is the match head side.

- Bet someone you can tie a napkin in a knot without letting go. Fold your arms before grabbing the ends of the napkin. Unfold your arms and the napkin will be tied.

- Drop a dime into an empty shot glass and bet that you can get the dime out without touching it or the glass. Lean in close and blow into the glass. The dime is so light that it will fly right out from your breath. You can even make a sexual innuendo by saying something like "See, all it takes is a good blow."

Learn to Play a Simple Song on Any Instrument

Be honest that it's all you know, which will actually impress people.

Learn to Draw One Cute Cartoon Character

This is one I did long ago. I don't have very good drawing ability, but I created a small, big-eyed cartoon character that tuned out pretty cute. I practiced and practiced, and I can draw it in under a minute. It's a great thing to add to the bottom of notes, or sometimes I'll even draw him on my bill at a restaurant, and I always get a reaction from the waitress.

You don't have to become a comic strip artist, but if you can create one signature character style, it's something you can quickly doodle on a napkin or in other fun places to bring a smile to her face.

Learn How to Say One Word in Various Languages

It could be something simple like how to order a beer in 20 languages or something sexier like

"You are the most beautiful woman I have ever seen."

And don't try to fake it, you'll get found out, and it will be incredibly embarrassing. Don't let Google translate (or another similar tool) be your guide. These are often inaccurate and can force you into making silly mistakes.

Learn the Constellations

Imagine you are walking along with a girl and you look up at the stars and can point out and name the constellations and the stories behind them. Just don't slip into professor lecture mode.

Learn How to Crack Eggs with One Hand

It sounds so simple, and it's actually pretty easy, but it looks so impressive.

Origami

This is one of those skills that is easy to learn, difficult to master. But if you can learn to make a few cool little animals, it is a fun little skill. However, don't be that guy who never stops. You don't want to be sitting at a table with your date and dozens of paper birds. That's not sexy.

Master Chopsticks

Once you get this down, you'll be part of the club with those who can use them and admired by those who cannot.

And women aren't impressed when you drop your food. But if you can crack a joke about it, then it can show how easy going you are and is a good way to show your sense of humor.

Pen Twirling and Coin Moving

I had a friend in high school who sat in the back of history class every day and worked on his pen twirling. Our teacher was pretty boring and didn't pay attention to what students would do, so Ernie would use this time to perfect this skill.

It took some time, but he got really good. Then he had a skill that he could use to impress and sometimes even punctuate his sentences. He would tell a joke and then twirl the pen at the end, almost like a rimshot for this joke. Girls really dug it.

You can do the same thing with flipping a coin between your fingers. It seems like such a simple thing, but when someone can't do it, they are always impressed. It's actually pretty good for nervous energy, but don't do it in front of her constantly.

In the next section, we are going to the field. And if you like what you've learned so far, or you've found benefit, feel free to leave a review on Amazon. I really appreciate it as your feedback means a lot to me.

Part Two: In the Field

Chapter 5: Wardrobe, Style, and Appearance

You've probably heard the saying "clothes make the man." While it can be taken a bit superficially, it is basically true. A man who dresses in his own style and has pride in themselves is always respected.

People react to you based on your appearance. If you look well put together and have pride in how you look, people and women will treat you differently. You will receive more respect and therefore be more successful. It radiates confidence and the sign of a man who knows how to be self-reliant.

On the flip side, someone who does not know how to take care of themselves, whether it be clothing or personal hygiene, is going to come across as slovenly and lacking of self-esteem.

So, which reaction would you rather have to your appearance?

Finding Your Own Style

Some guys have no problem developing their own style when it comes to their clothing and accessories. Sometimes I think they might go overboard, but hey, they have a style, and I totally support that.

When I talk about style, you don't have to become some identifiable stereotype or fashion model. It's just about knowing what clothes make you look good as well as whether or not you like the feel and enjoy wearing them.

We talked earlier about not being genuine. This isn't about taking on a persona. This is about finding your own vibe.

And let's clear something up, gentlemen, right here and now. Shorts, a baseball cap and flip-flops are not a style. I call it the "Frat Boy Look." This is not the look that most women are going to go for, especially if you are a few years post-college.

I did it, too, for all of college and a few years after. Flip flops and the ball cap turned backward. Then as I figured out how women react and listened to them, as well as growing out of it and moving into the real world, I developed my own style. I tend to not wear a lot of ties, going for an open-necked dress shirt, but I don't care for button-down collars. It's just not <u>my style</u>.

So, how do you figure out what is your own style?

- Start with what works for your body style. Don't wear something that just isn't made for you.

- Make sure it fits right. From suits to t-shirts, make sure it fits properly and doesn't pull or stretch in a strange way.

- Look for styles you like. Online, on television and in magazines. Look for celebrities who have the same body type as you. Look at what they wear and see if you like it.

- It doesn't need to happen every night.

- Again, it's a style, not a costume.

"But That Celebrity is Dressed Like a Homeless Person!"

Yes...but they are still a rich celebrity. Just because you are rich and famous doesn't mean you have style sense. Plus, that tabloid shot was them running to the grocery store to grab diapers in the middle of the night. Would you wear your most stylish stuff to do that?

Celebrities are great to see what they wear, but remember some of that is incredibly expensive and ultra-stylish. That means in a few months it's going to be out of style, and you wouldn't be caught dead wearing it. Also remember that a lot of them are dressed by people and provided clothes to wear.

Use some hints from them, but in the end, you need to develop your own unique style.

And in the end, always remember to take the weather and occasion into account. You might cut a dashing figure in a classic tuxedo, but if you wear it to a Fourth of July picnic, all you'll be getting is sweat soaking through your nice clothes for no good reason.

What Do Women Like in Clothing?

Of course, women have individual tastes. I dated one woman who absolutely loved this one shirt I had. The next woman I dated couldn't stand it.

However, there are some sort of universal things they do tend to like:

- Classic looks like a white (Clean!!!) t-shirt and jeans.

- Suits. Women love a good quality, well-fitted suit. The same thing goes for tuxedos.

- This one might sound strange, but it's true. Rolled-up sleeves. Remember I mentioned it earlier? Especially if you have good forearms.

- Nice shoes.

- Well-fitting jeans. No dad jeans, no baggy jeans... well, fitting jeans. Let's put it this way; you need to show off some goods, my friend. They like to see your assets as much as you do theirs. Note: keep in mind that we are talking about a well-fitting pair of jeans. Skinny jeans look as uncomfortable and painful to women as they must feel on you. Besides, no need to risk the family jewels needlessly.

What Do Women Not Like?

- White socks with black shoes. Same with those socks and sandals.

- Overuse of metal jewelry.

- Muscle shirts. If you're jogging, going to the gym, or participating in some other physical activity, they're fine. Otherwise, women would much rather not seen them. You don't want their nickname, "wife beaters", to stick with you because you wore one outside of exercise.

- Sweatpants in public.

- Crocks. Just don't.

- Flip Flops when you aren't at the beach. Same with Bermuda shorts.

- Speedos. Ever. Even at the pool and the beach.

- Light blue and all-white tuxedos. Stay out of the prom department.

- Pajamas in public. I know that sounds obvious, but I've heard of male college students showing up to lectures in pajama bottoms.

- Shorts and pants that sag below your butt. No one really likes it, actually. If you knew the prison origins of this style, you probably wouldn't, either.

- Repetition. They hate it when you always are wearing the same thing. They want to see your style.

Clothing Essentials

There are certain items that every man needs to have in their closet so that they are ready to be well dressed for any occasion.

A Suit

If you don't have one, buy one. Invest in a good quality suit. Just do it.

First of all, as a man, you need at one least one suit for weddings and funerals. Even if you don't have to wear one to work, you need one. You never want to be caught unaware for an event or a potential time to party and meet some women because you couldn't make the dress code.

If you can, get one light-colored and one dark-colored suit. This will give you some more options, especially in summer and warm weather.

A White Dress Shirt

You need a white dress shirt, not only for your suit, but it can be used for a number of looks. You can wear it with slacks for a semi-casual look or with jeans for the classic American look.

Classic Fit Jeans

Styles come and go, but nothing beats a classic fitted style pair of blue jeans.

Well-Made Leather Dress Shoes

Women notice shoes on men. It's one of those signs. They can tell a lot about not only the style but also the quality.

Sports Coat

Different than a suit, by just having a nice sports coat you can up your appearance instantly.

Underwear

New and clean. You never know who might see it. Studies have also discovered that women prefer boxer-brief trunk-style underwear.

A High-Quality White T-shirt

Some guys make the mistake of just throwing on an undershirt, which can work, but if you don't have an amazing body, those shirts can just look cheap and sloppy. Get a high-quality, white, 100% cotton t-shirt.

Shoes

When I was young, I learned a really important lesson. Women pay a lot of attention to shoes. No, not for the reason you are thinking, although a good share of women do subscribe to the big feet/big hands rule, but because they can tell a lot about you by how you wear your shoes.

- Always match your shoes and belt. It's a sign of well-put-together man.

- If they look cheap and flimsy, she might think the same about you.

- Sandals and flip-flops are not a fashion statement.

Physical Appearance and Hygiene

In my first ***How to Flirt with Women***, I discussed hygiene and taking care of yourself, basic things that we take for granted like showering, cleanliness, and presentation. This also includes taking care of your clothing and presentation. That definitely has not changed.

What woman is going to want to kiss you if you have a nasty smell coming from your mouth? Or cuddle up with you when you haven't showered for a few days? Most likely, she's not even going to want to talk to you.

- Brush your teeth, floss and use mouth-wash.

- Use deodorant.

- Shower at least once a day and clean every-where.

- Take care of your clothes and keep them clean.

- Stay in shape. Go to the gym regularly.

- Eat healthily and it will have an effect on your skin and help you with many blem-ishes and outbreaks.

- Keep your nails clean and trim.

- Check for any unsightly hairs on your back, neck or in your nose and trim them.

- Be careful with how much hairspray and hair gel you use. Too much can look unnatural and smells even worse.

- Ease up on the cologne and body spray. Seriously. Women don't want to taste your Axe when they open their mouths to talk to you.

Chapter 6: How to Build Confidence She Can See

It's one thing to say that women are attracted to confidence, but what if you have a problem with confidence? What if you are lacking in it?

The great thing about confidence is that it can be built and it's not that hard. You just need to create an environment where it can grow and develop in a healthy way.

How to Grow Your Confidence

Accomplish Things

This is probably the simplest way to build your confidence. It's simple, but it works for everyone.

Remember back when you were a kid and you were trying to learn to ride your bike? You didn't want to take those training wheels off because you didn't have the confidence you could keep that bike upright.

But after practice, some help from an adult and a leap of faith, those wheels came off, and you could ride unaided. So, you remember how confident you felt after that?

When you accomplish things, you become more confident, not only in that skill but across the board. You show yourself that you have skills and the ability to learn and you will use that confidence in other areas.

Work from the Outside-In

Dress yourself well and find your own personal style. I discussed this earlier, but it is just as important when it comes to your personal confidence. If you present yourself in a proper way, you will develop pride in your appearance, and that pride will, in turn, build your confidence.

People will compliment you, and that will also add to your confidence. You don't have to spend huge amounts of money on clothes and grooming supplies. Just learn what works for you and presents you in the best light.

Don't Compare Yourself to Other People

You are your own individual with your own strengths and weaknesses. You have your own dreams and accomplishments, and when you try to hold them up against other people, it's not fair to yourself. All that happens is you tear yourself down and your confidence suffers.

I was talking to one of my friends, and she was commenting on how hard it was to talk to someone who seemed to be comparing themselves to someone else. In one instance, she felt like the third wheel because the two men had been so preoccupied with trying to outshine each other that they barely let her get a word in edgewise.

Women do not want to see how you compare to others. They want to see who you are as a person, all on your own. The best thing to do is learn how to shut out the others in the room and focus on letting your originality shine out. Still at a loss? Put the focus on her, and you will really impress.

Take Care of Yourself

In order to have confidence, you have to be proud of yourself. You need to take care of yourself. Whether it's your physical appearance or your mental well-being, you need to take care of <u>you</u> first.

The healthier you are in mind and body, the more confident you will be that you can handle anything life throws at you.

Push Yourself

One way to build confidence is through doing things that you think you can't or that scare you. By pushing through and proving you can do it, you will gain more confidence in your abilities.

Try to do something every day that scares you. Look at your fears, whether they are rational or not, and challenge yourself. Do you not like being alone? Spend some time with yourself. Hate public speaking or talking to strangers? Force yourself to talk to someone new every day or get up in front of a group.

Track Your Progress

I love going to the gym and working out, but when I started going years ago, I didn't know what I was doing and started and stopped a few times before finally figuring out the exercise routine that worked for me.

Something I learned was that by charting my progress, I was much more successful and confident in my gym abilities. I could see not only what I had accomplished but also had proof of what I was capable of. So, when the little voice popped up and told me I couldn't do it, I had physical proof that not only could I do it, but I already had.

This can be used for any area where you are making progress. It doesn't have to be exercise. It can be hobbies, work or even dating. By tracking your progress, you'll become much more visibly confident in your skills.

Practice Speaking

If you can't get across what you are trying to say concisely and intelligently, people aren't going to respond, and your confidence is going to drop.

Practice speaking and telling stories. Once you can engage someone in conversation, you will have skills that mean you can always speak your mind and move toward your goals. This will add to your confidence and resonate with those you speak with, especially women.

Practice throughout the day. Make small talk in the elevator. Strike up a conversation with the guy behind the counter at a convenience store. Try telling them a quick joke. Every time you interact with someone, you gain confidence.

Focus on Your Good Qualities

It's easy to fall into the practice of putting ourselves down. Usually, it's out of fear of being cocky. After all, aren't we supposed to praise modesty?

Yes, but that doesn't mean we shouldn't ever acknowledge, even celebrate, our positive qualities. Yet doing so can make us feel better and raise our confidence. Not to mention it can get annoying when people say that they can't find anything nice to say about themselves.

So, get into the practice of writing down at least three of your positive qualities each day. For example, one of your qualities could say, "I have a giving heart." Easy as that. Preferably, write it out by hand rather than typing or on your smartphone. The physical act of writing it by hand will reinforce the message for you, as will reading it out loud.

This will feel a bit silly at first, but after a while, you'll start to enjoy it. As you continuously remind yourself of your good qualities, you will start to see yourself in a more positive light. As a result, your confidence will grow.

Be Positive

As a rule, negative people aren't overly confident. They usually rely on basic skills and getting by because they are too busy complaining.

Stay positive about yourself and the world. If you need extra help, you can always use positive affirmations or mantras. Choose a theme for the day that is positive and you can work on. Maybe get a book of daily affirmations or a calendar. Every morning read one and take it with you as you start your day.

Use your social media presence to put out positive vibes. The more you feel a lack of confidence or down, push in the opposite direction toward people on social media and be an instrument for positivity.

Weave this into your actions. Not only will you be positive but will have achieved something and gained even more confidence.

Confidence with Women

You may be feeling right now that you have confidence, but it's just when you are around women that you don't. You know what? That's normal, too.

I've known people in the corporate world who could run huge companies, stand in front of thousands of people and give inspirational speeches, but when you put them in a one-on-one situation with a woman, they freeze and have no idea how to act. All the confidence they showed in the rest of their life is suddenly gone.

This isn't a bad thing. In fact, it's great because you know exactly what to work on.

So how do you build your confidence, specifically with women?

Here are two approaches:

- Take it one step at a time. Don't throw yourself in the deep end. You need to learn to walk before you can run. Don't expect to be a world-class conversationalist with a woman in a matter of minutes. You need to build up. Maybe just start with a few lines and how to open up a conversation. It will come quickly, but you need to build the foundation of confidence.

- The other approach is sort of a machine gun way. By talking to every woman you meet and getting used to interacting and seeing how easy and well it can go, your confidence will grow.

It really depends on your personality and style. Some people have near-crippling anxiety or lack of confidence when it comes to women and might need an approach that is a bit less shocking, while others need that 180 turn in order to kick their confidence into high gear. It depends on your personality and situation.

It is important to remember that there is a difference between confidence and being condescending or pushy. I don't know how many times some of my friends would tell me they didn't like a guy because he seemed so cocky and full of himself, only to find out later the guy had just been trying to fake confidence!

Confidence is a hard one to fake. You need to be able to really work on feeling it, not just faking it. And don't let it go overboard. No woman wants to be belittled or feel like they are beneath you in the process.

I would highly suggest that you go for the machine style and talk to every single woman that you want to. You'll shock your confidence higher just through practice.

Chapter 7: The First Date

You talked to her, you both laughed together, and you got her number. Now it's time for the first date.

So, what do you need to do to make it a success?

Be You

Make sure that you are not trying to put on an act or suddenly try to impress her on the date.

Some guys think that now that there is a block of a few hours that they will be with the girl, they need to tell them stories, impress them with numerous activities on a single date. No! **Just be yourself.**

Keep It Light

No matter how much of a connection you may have, you don't want to fall into heavy topics like past or future relationships. Never go into a monologue about your ex or start talking about the future family you want to have.

Keep it fun and light. Don't let the topics get too heavy, but that doesn't mean you have to stay out of deep conversations.

Keep It Simple

Don't plan a multitude of things that you are going to do. You don't want to plan a movie, dinner, going out afterward and possibly throwing in plans for coffee and dessert.

It can be stressful just going on a first date, and while all of these things are fun, you don' want them to overshadow the time you are spending together. While you want to do something fun, you want to be able to talk and get to know each other as well.

There are a lot of great things that you can do on the first date to get them interested and to give you two the time to talk. Some of these include:

1. Going on a picnic in the park. Doing this at night while you watch the sun set can be particularly amazing.

2. Going to the library and checking out each other's favorite book.

3. Meeting up for coffee (this helps to keep things more casual).

4. Walk around the farmer's market.

5. If you know that she likes to be out in nature, consider taking her to the nearest state park. There is fishing, swimming, hiking, and so much to explore. Stay out late and enjoy looking at the stars together, too.

6. Have a cooking night. If you are nervous about how to split the check, invite her over to your house and make her dinner. You can be the romantic and make the meal or make it a group activity where you cook together.

7. Visit a museum. No matter where you live, there is likely to be some kind of museum around to check out. Try to find one out of the way or one with interesting and unique things she hasn't seen before.

8. Wine tasting. You can take her on an organized wine tour or just visit some local wineries, whether alone or with a group.

You should be careful about a few places, especially on a first date. A movie might be fun, but it doesn't give the two of you much time to talk. And a fancy restaurant is a very thoughtful idea, but it does make you both feel nervous, and you won't have time to socialize.

One thing to note is about paying for the date. Traditionally, the man would pay for the meal and any activities. This would show that he could be a provider and take care of the woman.

Today, it kind of depends on the woman. Some women still find this attractive and will have no problem with it. Others might be uncomfortable having someone pay for them or might be too independent to allow for this. Taking charge and asking which they feel the most comfortable with is a good way to show that you really care about their feelings.

Do this before the date. If you would like to be the one who pays, let them know this ahead of time. Then, if it is a big deal to them, they can let you know before the date comes and a heated discussion starts up. Since this is the first date, be open to either option and let the woman have the choice on which way things will go.

Group Dates and Group Outings

If you are nervous, consider going out on a group date or outing. The pressure can be less because there are other people around.

However, be clear that you are on a date and not just going as a group. As the event moves on, try to find alone time away from the crowd where the two of you can connect.

What to Talk About on a First Date

You are both a bit nervous, so the conversation might be a bit strange and forced at first. You want to get to know her, but what do you ask?

You want to ask interesting things that get the two of you talking, but you don't want to get too personal right away.

Try some of these topics:

- **"If you could get a plane right now and go anywhere, where would you go?"**

    This is a great question because it's different than the usual travel questions. It lets you get to know the places where she would like to travel but also the mindset she is in that minute. If she is in need of a vacation, she might say somewhere relaxing. If she's feeling romantic in the moment, she might say somewhere like Paris.

- **"Growing up, did you have a nickname?"**

This is informative and fun. You get to learn a little bit about her childhood, but you also might get a fun and personal story about her.

- **"What is on your Bucket List?"**

We all have them. Those things we want to accomplish before we "kick the bucket." Some of them might be big while others might be smaller but no less important. This gives you a great place to talk and maybe come up with some ways to help her cross some off her list or maybe yours.

- **"What scares you?"**

This is an excellent question because it will cause her to open up. She is letting you know her fears, so make sure you earn her trust by not belittling her. Share your own, so she feels safe having told you.

- **"What is a song that you could listen to over and over and over?"**

  Music can be very emotional, and often there are songs that we love because they are connected to wonderful moments in our lives. Asking her about a song that means a lot to her will help her open up. Most likely she will tell you the story behind it, and you will grow a bit closer.

Then there are always the old go-to questions:

- **"If you were stranded on a desert island, what three things would you being? Or what food or album?"**

- **"What's your ultimate dream job?"**

- **"If you won the lottery, what would you do with the money?"**

- **"If you could have dinner with anyone from history alive or dead, who would it be?"**

- **"What is the worst pick-up line someone has ever used on you?"**

- **"What type of movies and TV shows do you enjoy? How about music and books?"**

Topics to Avoid

In *How to Talk to Women*, I discuss extensively how to have great conversations, how to steer them and how to create chemistry while you are talking. I also extensively discuss topics to avoid in conversations. For more information, check it out.

Here are a few subjects to definitely avoid:

Money

It's probably a bit early to start telling her how much you make, what you like to spend your money on or your plans for retirement. It's also none of your business how much she makes. Eventually down the road, you'll talk about it (and really should before you get into a relationship) but for now, stay off the subject.

Ideal Women

I can't believe guys do this (and women, too). They'll get a date with an amazing woman, and instead of learning about her, they'll spout off what they are looking for in a woman, no matter what she has going for her. They'll say things about how they like this or that, or a certain appearance or type, all of which they don't know if it's her.

This is incredibly rude and disrespectful. You are on a date with her, so give her all your attention. At that moment, as far as you should be concerned, there are no other women in the world.

Politics and Religion

Until you know where you both stand, be very careful on these topics. You don't want to have a wonderful date ruined because you said something offhand about her beliefs.

Your Exes

It's going to come up, but don't dwell on it. She wants to hear about you, not the women you've dated.

Sexual History

Like your exes, this will come up eventually, but the first date is not the time. It could make an otherwise nice evening very awkward. Someone will most likely end up feeling judged, either for being too experienced or not being experienced enough, and that won't get you anywhere. If you seem to be heading towards spending the night together, then you'll want to have this conversation before you go through with it. Otherwise, it's not necessary yet.

When the topic does finally come up, be honest. You can't have a strong, healthy relationship if you lie about something like this. If you've only had one partner or even if you're a virgin, tell her. If she judges you for that, she's not the kind of person you'll want to be with and it's good that you find that out now. On the flip side, if you've slept with a lot of women, tell her that, too, but don't brag about it. Don't fake modesty, either. That's just another way of bragging without admitting you're bragging. Either way, the date will end a lot earlier than you'd like if you approach the topic that way.

Your Future Together

I've noticed an irritating trend among younger generations lately. It seems that rather than having the "going out" or "going on dates" stage, in which two people get to know each other and are open to going on dates with other people as well with no real commitment, the first date immediately sends a couple into the "dating" or "boyfriend/girlfriend" stage. Next thing you know, they'll be talking about their future together.

Sounds a bit ridiculous, right? Maybe even a bit disconcerting?

That's exactly what it would sound like if you started talking about a hypothetical future with a woman on your first date. It seems a bit outrageous that anyone would do this, but both men and women are guilty of it. No matter who starts it, typically, it freaks the other person out. That's when their first date also becomes their last date. Do yourself a favor and don't get ahead of yourself.

Right Location

People seem to think that you have to stick to a certain rotation of location types when it comes to first dates: movie theaters, fast casual or fancy restaurants, cafés, and so forth. However, that simply isn't true. The exact location itself does not really matter. Heck, one of my favorite first dates was eating McDonald's in my car while watching raindrops hit the river. No, what it all boils down to is how well the location helps you get to know your date.

It doesn't have to be dinner, either. Maybe coffee is good enough because you are both busy. Plus, that way you can make sure there's a good connection before you lay out the cash for dinner.

Make sure you pick somewhere nice and not too loud. Concerts, clubs, and bowling alleys, for instance, might get too loud for you to have any worthwhile conversation. At the same time, you won't want to pick somewhere where silence is expected, either. Movies are considered a dating classic and the woman you've asked out might really want to check out that new Picasso exhibit, but both movie theaters and museums expect a certain level of quiet, so getting to know each other will be next to impossible.

Pick somewhere that shows her you listened to her during your last conversation. Did she mention spending a summer abroad in Italy? Take her to that nice Italian restaurant by your office. Is she a tea drinker through-and-through? Consider taking her to a teahouse rather than an ordinary café. Does she love nature? Pack a couple of sandwiches and some water and spend the day in the park. Don't pick a place where you'll be absolutely miserable just to please her, but show her that you put some effort into choosing somewhere that you thought she would enjoy.

Don't go somewhere you have brought other dates, especially if it's a place you and an old girlfriend used to frequent. I would stay away from restaurants that you haven't been to at all unless there's a really good review online.

And remember, you don't have to pay a small fortune for a first date. Honestly, a lot of women will feel uncomfortable if you spend too much on them at first, partly out of humility and partly out of the cultural precedent that guys who do that expect something in return. (You can thank many jerks who came before you for that particular issue.) Most women will just want to have fun and spend time getting to know you. If she does put up a fuss because she doesn't think you spent enough, well, then it's best you find that out now and cut her loose before it gets too serious.

How to Tease and Flirt

For the best knowledge, go read my book **_How to Flirt with Women_**. The entire volume is devoted to ways to break the ice, start a conversation, be confident and tons of other great ways. Here are a few highlights specifically for a first date:

- Try some fun innuendo. Maybe take something she said wrong as if it was sexual and give her a hard time about it.

- Touching is very important, but make sure you do it at the right time. Try to punctuate a story by touching her hand.

- Try teasing her a bit. It could be about something she said or something she did. Don't be cruel but be playful and fun.

- When you tell her stories about your life, make sure they are fun and you tell them well. If you tell jokes, make sure they are funny and appropriate.

- Make sure to keep eye contact during your date.

- Try mimicking her for fun, but don't go too far with it.

Asking for the Second Date

First of all, always go for the second date before you say goodnight. You might not have the exact activity or time, but you need to know that she wants to see you again. Try your best, however, to get something specific.

It doesn't have to be formal. Try saying something like "we should do this again sometime." If she answers affirmatively, then don't hesitate. Set something up right then. She'll see you are serious and most likely say yes.

If she says no or we'll see, I'll have to be honest with you, you probably aren't going to see each other again. Most likely, you probably picked that up earlier, but that's going to be for sure.

At the End of the Date

The night is winding down. You both had a great time, and you're getting ready to say goodbye. So how should it go?

Be Thankful

Let her know you had a good time and that you are thankful she went out with her. You don't need to gush and repeat yourself over and over but let her know you enjoyed yourself. A sincere "Thank you" can go a long way.

Make Sure She's Getting Home Safely

You may have picked her up, or she may have driven to the location or taken a rideshare. However she got there, it's your responsibility as a man to make sure she gets home safely.

Offer to drive her home if she didn't drive. If she did, make sure you offer to walk her to her car.

When to Kiss Her

OK, now this might not be the answer you want to hear, but it's the truth.

You should know most of the time.

Told you it wasn't the answer, but it's true. In **How to Talk to Women**, I mentioned something called The Spark. It's that electricity that you feel when two people are attracted to each other. Some people call it chemistry or sexual energy, but it's just the feeling two people get when they are into each other.

Most often, as you are standing there at the end of the date, you are going to feel it. So, if you do, lean in and kiss her. Most likely she's going to meet you halfway there.

Often, women will kiss someone they are sort of into but not completely connected to, but that doesn't mean you should take advantage of it. Don't go in with a big open mouth and stick your tongue down her throat.

One thing about kissing is that it can be a test. She may just want to get a little taste to see how you handle yourself or if you know what you are doing.

So, don't have expectations. Be in the moment and enjoy it.

Honestly, if you feel the spark, you don't have to wait until after the date. One of the exciting things is those little moments where you get close and accidentally brush up against each other, and your lips are mere inches apart. Very often this will turn into a kiss, and the date isn't even half over.

That's always great because it leads to more kissing and the stress of do you connect is now over. The chemistry is boiling, and things are going great.

Sex on the First Date

I've always been honest with you, right? Well, here I go again. Sex does happen on a first date, but not that often and, honestly, you don't really want it to happen.

If you are just looking to score, then, by all means, go for it. The next chapter is all about having sex. But if you are looking to develop a meaningful relationship, I highly suggest you don't even think about it. You can joke and work toward having a sexually charged date and maybe even mess around a bit before you go home, but I would save the sex for a few dates down the line.

Above all, never expect sex on a first date or any date. Honestly, even when you are in a relationship, don' t expect sex. When you set expectations, it isn't fair to the woman, and you are really just setting yourself up for potential disappointment. It doesn't mean you didn't want her or want sex or plan on pursuing it. Just don't expect that you are entitled to it.

Afterward

Don't pretend you are interested if you aren't. Be honest but nice. Don't tell her you'll call if you don't plan on it.

If you like her, call or text, but don't smother her or do it too much and come across as needy. It's ok to send a pleasant text after the date saying how much fun you had and you look forward to seeing her again.

Make sure to set the details for your next date right away. Try to see if you can do something on a night where you don't have to worry about when you are wrapped up.

Chapter 8: Sex

It's what we are all looking for, right? You may be the type of man who needs it almost every day and will be happy to have sex with any woman, or you might be a bit more selective for physical or emotional reasons. It doesn't matter. Eventually, we all want to have sex. I'm guessing that's a big reason you picked up this book.

Know Your Sex Ed

It's hard to believe, but it seems like there's an increasing number of men who either didn't pay attention in sex ed classes, had cruddy ones or were exempt from them altogether. They don't seem to know a lick about female anatomy, sex or safe sex.

Some of them barely know about their own anatomy.

I remember talking to this one guy on Twitter who genuinely thought that women could hold their periods in and choose when they happen. Seriously. He thought that feminine products were unnecessary because they could just "wait until they got to the bathroom if they wanted to". I am perfectly comfortable in my masculinity and gender identity, but that is the closest I've ever come to being ashamed of being a man.

Please, brush up on your sex ed before actually hitting the sack with someone. Why is that important? Because if you don't understand how it works, there is no way that you'll actually be good at it. Even if you know roughly what will make you feel good, if you don't understand or properly remember sex ed, you won't be able to figure out what will make her feel good. Trust me, it's a lot better when you can both enjoy it.

Women will also be more attracted to you if you know your stuff in this area. It might not come up often in conversation, but if it does, looking informed is the much better option. Otherwise, you don't look like just a moron, you look like a misogynistic pig.

Safety First

Ok, guys, you've had this drilled into your head since you noticed your first girl. Be safe. You don't want to catch something or, even more, have little versions of you running around out there. In all seriousness, part of being a real man is acting responsibly and protecting yourself and your partners. Be a man.

Condom

Always wear a condom unless you are in a committed relationship. Even then, make sure that you have discussed birth control and your thoughts on what to do if the unexpected happens.

Get tested regularly. Even if you practice safe sex, get yourself tested regularly for sexually transmitted diseases.

Don't Believe the Myths

There are some myths about ways in which you can keep a girl from getting pregnant without protection. One of the most prominent and well-known ways is called "pulling out", in which the man pulls out right before the big moment. The problem is that there's no guarantee that this will prevent pregnancy. In fact, there's no proof that any of a number of myths will work. Since you're a grown adult, I suggest cutting through all of the hoopla and just going with the tried and true: condoms, birth control, sponges, and other kinds of contraceptives.

No Stealthing

"Stealthing" is when a man will put on a condom at the beginning of sex, often at the woman's request, and then remove it sometime during without telling her. Often, the woman won't find out until she finds out that she has an STD or she's pregnant.

Now, most men won't do this. It's a cowardly and jerk thing to do. Still, there are a few men out there who will try and make women distrust all men even more. Just because it feels better to you without the condom does not mean it's the right thing to do. Think big picture, and respect the woman you're with enough to wear a condom if that's what she wants.

Putting It in Isn't the Only Way You Can Get Something

This isn't the most fun topic, but the cold hard truth is you can get diseases from oral sex, both giving and receiving. Probably the most common of this type is herpes. While it isn't sexy, take into consideration using condoms or dental dams during oral sex.

This is one of those reasons to start talking to women about sexual history before sleeping with them. You have to make an effort to protect yourself with knowledge.

Virginity

It's also possible that you picked up this book and you are a virgin. You have never had sex before and don't know what to do, expect or how to proceed. What do you do to get the opportunity to have sex? Is something wrong because you haven't yet?

First of all... nothing is wrong with you. There are people who have stayed virgins for years and those who lost it when they were teenagers. Everyone is different.

Is It a Choice or Circumstance?

Some people make a choice to wait to have sex until it's with someone they care about or love or maybe even until marriage. It's a personal choice, but honestly, it's one a lot of people make in their teens or early 20s and then end up changing their minds.

If you think you are a virgin by circumstance, that you can't find a woman who will have sex with you, that's garbage. There will always be a woman out there who will have sex with you. Always. The question is, do you want to have sex with her? I'm guessing there have been numerous opportunities for you to have sex, but you probably didn't realize they were out there. It's not circumstantial, it's a choice you made.

Should You Tell the Woman?

This is a tough one, but my initial answer would be no, with a caveat.

I don't believe that you should volunteer the information. It shouldn't come out in conversation. "Well, I was born in Boston. I like football oh and I'm a 26-year-old virgin."

Yeah, not a good idea.

However, if it comes up naturally and you are feeling a connection with her, it's ok to tell her. But don't dwell on it. Don't tell her you feel strange about it, or like you are missing something. Just say the right opportunity hasn't come up yet and leave it at that.

I would highly suggest that you tell her after the fact, if you didn't already. You don't want her to think that you are inexperienced. She will actually be happier to know that she is your first and will actually want to have sex with you more to teach you what she knows and see what you can learn together.

What if I'm Bad at It?

Sex is not something like you see in the movies. You always see it go perfectly, no one pulls on each other's hair, no one puts things where they shouldn't go, everyone looks great afterward.

Sex can be messy, full of mistakes and problems even with the most experienced participants — especially the first time together. So, don't worry.

Can She Tell I've Never Had Sex?

Well, the sure way she'll figure it out is if you tell her.

For the most part, no, she's not going to know. In fact, most guys who have little experience tend to brag more about it. And women know this.

As for the actual act, odds are she's going to be a little nervous because it's your first time together. She wants to have fun but most likely has her own insecurities and fears. So as long as you don't do something fundamentally wrong like trying to put it in her ear, she's not going to be worried it's your first time.

She may think you are inexperienced (which you are), but as I said above, you should tell her afterward.

But What if You Know... It's Over Really Quickly?

It sucks. And it happens to every guy.

Be honest with her. Explain it was your first time. As long as you don't get weird or cry or something, she's going to understand. And if she doesn't, it's ok. Her real personality is coming out, and you are seeing it.

If you notice it's becoming a problem, then you might need to start working on your technique or mental place in order to make it last longer. Try different positions and ways of having sex that doesn't push you toward the end so quickly. There's always thinking of baseball scores.

Honestly, when you get more experienced and are with someone you have a connection with, you will last just the right amount of time.

Initiating Sex

Sex usually just happens. It isn't planned, at least by the couple. It's usually just when the build-up is right; the time has come.

If you are already kissing and moving toward it, then just let it progress. However, at some point, she may push back. Be very aware of what she is saying to you.

When She Initiates It

I will admit, sometimes us men can be a little oblivious when women are the ones trying to initiate sex. Women can be much more subtle with their advances. When you combine that with not wanting to make any assumptions, women's advances can go right over our heads.

Shortly out of college, I started seeing an older woman named Miriam. We didn't sleep together right away, so I figured that Miriam wanted to take things slow. On the fourth date, she invited me to her place since her sons were with their dad for the week. After dinner, we snuggled up on the couch to watch a movie on Netflix. We kissed a bit but nothing too serious. Suddenly, Miriam draped her leg over mine, causing her short, *short* dress to ride up. Then, she started running her hand over my chest. The nail in the coffin—what really should have driven her point home—was when she gave me a kiss on the neck. And what did I do?

Nothing. Just like a moron, I smiled at her, kissed her forehead and then returned to watching the movie with her all over me. Fortunately, Miriam, being an older woman—the praises of which I sing in *How to Flirt with Women*—knew not to play these games long and finally just kissed me full on the lips. Things progressed naturally from there.

Afterward, Miriam admitted to me that she had been trying to "seduce" me (her words), and I admitted that I had no clue at all. After we shared a good laugh at my expense, Miriam shared one of many valuable lessons that she taught me in our relationship: most women will be subtle about sex. They'll be *sensual*, she explained, not overtly sexual.

I knew from that day on the kinds of things to look out for when a woman is trying to initiate sex.

- Touch. She'll stroke your chest or your arm, touch the inside of your leg, run her hand along your jaw. She's trying to stimulate the both of you through touch. And I'll admit, it's a pretty good turn-on.

- Proximity. Sometimes being close to you really is just cuddling and wanting to be close to you. She wraps her leg around you, though, it might mean something more. You'll have to watch for other signs to be sure.

- Speech. Is she speaking unusually low and breathy? It could be a sign of sexual arousal.

- Exposing skin. If she's purposefully letting her clothes move to expose her skin, this could mean that she's inviting you to touch her. Be very careful with this one, though. Her skin could just be showing with no real intention behind it, so be certain to look for other signs first before trying anything. If you've been dating long enough to be comfortable with each other, test the waters by playfully pulling the clothes back down and teasing her about it.

- Kissing. This one is pretty obvious. If she's really going at it with the kissing, sex might be on the way. Mind you, she could just be looking for a good make out session, which can also be fun, but don't be surprised if it goes the sex route instead.

Now, even if the woman initiates it, it does not mean that she has to follow through. Sure, it could be annoying to feel teased like that, but it is her choice. Even if you're in the middle of the act, if she tells you she wants to stop or otherwise indicates that she wants to stop, **stop**. Just because she started it, doesn't mean she has to see it through.

Complete Refusal

This is a woman who you are not going to change her mind. It could be she's not attracted to you in a way you can't change. You need to respect her. Besides, at a certain point, your begging for sex is really going to turn her off.

The upside is there aren't very many of these women out there. One of the major lies in the world is that women don't want to have sex. Of course, they do.

A Partial Resistance

The two of you are making out and having fun, but she has drawn a line in the sand and won't allow you to cross. But she still wants to play around. It might still happen, but she has to really let you know it's ok before you move in.

Token Resistance

This is a term that has popped up in the last few years. It means she's resisting you because that what she's expected to do.

You can usually tell when this is in play because she might say something along the lines of "We shouldn't be doing this" as she does exactly that. One move that happens a lot is that she'll stop you for a moment and then throw herself into you with even more heated passion.

Women don't want to come across as giving it away and want to make you work a little bit for it. This is part of the game, and if you read the signs wrong, she is going to tell you it's time to go home, and you won't understand why.

Here's my thought on the subject. I either want to, or I don't. I don't want to play this game of back and forth. So, I will respectfully say you know what, it's time for me to go. I look forward to when we are at a point when we're ready to have sex.

You need to make your own decision, but no matter what, respect her boundaries.

Why Won't She Have Sex with Me?

She Doesn't Completely Trust You

A woman needs to trust you to really give herself to you physically. Some women can fake it, but if you are looking for something deeper, you should really respect that she needs more before she can have sex with you.

There Isn't Enough Sexual Tension

It's just not right. It was fun to kiss you, but it's just not enough to get her to want to have sex with you.

You don't want pity sex, so call it a night.

She's Concerned About Consequences

You might work together, know the same people or she might be worried about how this will affect your relationship. It's the whole "what will you think of me in the morning" issue.

Depending on how long you have been dating, you might need to have a discussion about what she needs to feel safe with you. And after sex, make sure you don't turn your back on the assurances you might have given her.

Never promise to be with her forever or other lofty, unobtainable goals. After people fight, they say, "Let's never fight again," but they know they are going to do it.

People change, and you don't know what's going to happen in a couple of years. Always make assurances in the here and now about things that you really can follow through on — things like your character and masculine values.

A Tale of Sex Gone Wrong

When I was in college, I had a good friend named Sammy that had worked his way up from a low-income family and neighborhood and gotten a full-ride scholarship to our university. He got good grades, was a great guy and had a very bright future.

One night at a party, he met a girl and they hit it off. They ended up having sex, and everything seemed great.

Then, a few weeks later, the girl went to the school administration and told them that Sammy had raped her. She said that she had tried to stop him and Sammy had forced himself on her.

We were all shocked. We had known Sammy for years, and this totally wasn't the type of thing he would do. He respected women and was that type of guy. He could never have done this.

However, the school investigated and based upon what the girl told them, Sammy was suspended pending an investigation.

This caused him to lose his scholarship, and he had to leave school during the investigation because he couldn't pay for classes or rent or food. He had to get a job, and the only place he could go was back to his old neighborhood while the investigation continued.

It dragged on for months, and finally, the girl admitted that he didn't rape her, that she just felt guilty for having a one-night stand. It rocked the school. Everyone was talking about it and how our friend Sammy had been exonerated.

But for Sammy, it was too late. He couldn't get his scholarship back and couldn't afford school without it. He had to get a low-paying job and, the last I heard, he was working in a man's clothing store trying to make ends meet.

The reason I'm telling you this story is because you need to realize that you need to be very careful about consent and reading signs. There are even some schools who have gone as far as requiring written consent before students have sex.

Look, I'm not trying to take the fun out of sex, I'm just explaining how a responsible man needs to approach it. Part of being accountable is about not putting yourself in situations where you can get into trouble. It's not just about pressuring her too far but also about being in situations where things could be taken wrong. You need to always be aware and be observant of signs.

If the woman has had more than a few glasses of anything, just don't have sex, even if she seems interested or acts like she wants to. People don't make the same decisions when they are sober as they do when drunk. It is much better to be on the safe side (and possibly have her mad at you for the night) than to do something and have her feel like she was taken advantage of by you.

You Don't Need to Know Why

Some men think that just because they've been denied sex that they have a right to know why. The hard truth is **you don't**.

Whatever reason a woman has for resisting sex is her own. Sex is a very personal experience, and what a woman wants to do with her body is her choice.

There are any number of reasons why a woman won't choose to have sex with you, many of which have no bearing on you whatsoever. She might have just gotten out of a bad relationship. Heaven forbid, she might be working through some trauma related to sexual abuse. And she might just not be in the mood. You don't know what she's been through before, and you don't know what she's going through now. Maybe someday she'll trust you enough to let you in on why she held off, but until then, it's none of your business.

Resistance to Sex

Ok, this is a tough one, because remember... **No means No**.

Resistance to sex doesn't mean that she's not into you or even interested in having sex, but you need to respect her and what she says.

Foundation for Later

There could be reasons she doesn't want to have sex right now, and no matter what you do, you aren't going to change her mind.

Men don't like to talk about it, but she could be having her period. So honestly, sex is not going to happen (contrary to popular belief, most women aren't fans of bloody sex, and the idea of Red Wings grosses them out). So, you can push all you want, but all you are going to do is annoy her.

She might mention that's why she held off, but probably not until you guys are already moving down that road.

How to Have Great Sex

OK, I'm not going to give you a lesson about human sexuality. You know what goes where and how the entire process works. If not, I suggest you go pick up a biology book and watch some porn.

What I can offer you are some ways to make it great.

My first piece of advice... don't ask "Do you like that?" over and over and over.

There Is No Such Thing as Normal... but Make Sure She's into It

There is an entire spectrum of sexual acts that people are into. Some people like a little bondage while others like a lot. Some women absolutely can't stand to be spanked while others absolutely love it and will scream for more.

Everybody is wired differently, and some of the fun of sex is figuring out what you both like.

I would highly suggest not getting into "other stuff" during your first time together. If she asks for something, by all means, give her what she wants. Most likely that first time it'll be a little playful slapping or some dirty talk. As you get further into the relationship, you can talk about what you're into or curious about.

Note: Don't suggest a threesome. Most girls aren't into them, and honestly, they aren't all they are cracked up to be.

You Aren't a Porn Star

Don't try to replicate every position you've seen in porn. And don't think you have to perform at that level. Sex should be fun, but intimate. You don't need to try to recreate the Kama Sutra.

What many people don't understand is that an average 20 minutes pro scene can take an entire day and several sessions to film. The average male porn star will have an orgasm; they give him a few minutes and keep shooting. He could have half a dozen during the course of shooting.

Often, they are also using Viagra or other enhancement drugs. Having sex for a half hour isn't the norm.

Don't worry about changing things up and trying to dazzle her. Just be there with her in the moment, and you'll be fine.

Listen

Listen to the way she reacts. When you do certain things, does she moan more? Does she make different noises? Does she tell you not to stop?

Also, silence isn't always a bad thing. I have been with several women who would become completely silent for a bit before they had intense orgasms. Sometimes if you are doing it so right, they actually have to pull themselves together enough to make noise during orgasms.

What if It's Her First Time?

Just like it might be your first time, it could be her first time, too. She might not tell you it's her first time, either, and you might not realize it until the deed is already done. If she does let you know, don't panic. First of all, it's a good sign. It means that she trusts you enough both to be her first time and to let you know that it's her first time.

Second, it's still possible to have great sex in this case. It just takes a lot of care and consideration.

Here are some pointers for how to have great and safe sex when it's her first time:

- Be gentle. A woman's first time can be very painful even under the best circumstances, so don't be too rough.

- Be patient. She might start to have second thoughts partway through. If that's the case, don't try to pressure her into continuing. She might decide to keep going despite her hesitation. If she doesn't, she'll appreciate you respecting her choice, which will lay the foundation for solid relationship in the future.

- Listen to her. I don't just mean listen to what she might say, although obviously if she says something during sex, you should pay attention. What I really mean is to listen to her body. Pay attention to how she reacts to certain things. If her body reacts positively to something, take note of it. She reacts negatively, don't do it.

- There will be a mess afterwards. Don't get embarrassed or embarrass her over it. Just wash the sheets, maybe look online for any tricks as to how to get the stains out. You might even want to put a towel down beforehand so that the blood and other fluids get on there instead.

- Most importantly, make sure she's okay. While there will inevitably be some pain, there will be a point when it will just be too much for her, and that's when you need to stop and check on her. She might be too embarrassed to tell you, so be her advocate. Let her know that you won't be mad if she needs to stop. After all, the sex won't truly be great if someone is in pain the whole time or if something goes horribly wrong.

If She's Doing Something You Don't Like, Let Her Know

Most likely, she is using skills she learned from her experiences and what men have told her they like. Well, it doesn't mean that you are going to like it. So, tell her nicely what feels good. Try to guide her instead of barking orders.

Or she might just open you up to a whole new pleasure. Keep an open mind.

After

If it's your first time together, don't jump up and run out, but be honest if you have to leave. If you are at your place, don't do something that makes her feel not welcome.

Part Three: In A Relationship

Chapter 9: From Dating to A Relationship

So, this is the point where I know you are stopping and saying "Wait a minute, what do <u>you</u> know about relationships? You're all about flirting and meeting women."

Well, I'm going to blow your mind. Ready?

I was married and got divorced. And it was one of the most successful relationships of my life.

My wife and I were married for seven years, and they were great. And yes, we got divorced, and that was painful, but because we communicated, we knew it was time. Nobody cheated, no one was in the wrong; it was just two people who realized that they wanted different things.

Thanks to the nature of our relationship, we were able to know when it was time to call it quits.

So, I do know how to have a successful relationship. Although my marriage ended, I don't see it as a failure. It ended on good terms and we are good friends.

The One

So, what happens when you reach that point where you are meeting women, but you want something a bit more? You want to meet someone to have a relationship with, maybe even get married.

It happens, and it's all part of dating.

What is The One to You?

You need to sit down and figure out exactly what you are looking for in a relationship. If you don't, you could easily get into something and wake up a few years down the road thinking "How the hell did I get here?"

Ask yourself some questions:

- Am I ready to be monogamous?

- Do I want to have children?

- Is religion an issue to me?

- Do I have the time for a relationship right now?

- Do I have plans for the future that I don't want to change?

- What am I unwilling to accept?

- What importance is sex in a relationship?

- What do I find attractive and unattractive in a woman?

- What values are important to me in a woman?

- What am I willing to make concessions on in a relationship and not?

Avoiding Women That Aren't Right

You are going to come across a lot of women who aren't right for you before you find your one. The easiest way to avoid them is to buy making sure you get to know them early on, so you don't waste your time and emotions on the wrong girl.

Don't be overly critical, but be honest with yourself about them during the first date, or even when you first meet them. Use the list you compiled to see if they are what you are looking for.

Don't hyper-focus on things or waiver from your core values over a pretty face, but there will be some give and take. You have to decide how much to give for you to remain a self-reliant man.

How Do You Know It's Getting Serious?

Relationships are different for everyone. Sometimes they sneak up on you, and for others, they knew it was right from the first moment they met. However, there are always signs that you can look for to know that this is heading toward something deeper and meaningful.

You Can't Keep Your Hands Off Each Other

I'm not talking about sex because sex is something that goes up and down in a relationship. You won't always be in the mood, life can cause distractions, or just over time, it starts to fade a bit. Lust is also different. Without enough connections other than physical, it'll only to be so deep.

This is about holding hands and kissing. Or some playful touching or PDAs. You have no problem with the world knowing this is someone you are interested in. You feel a connection when you touch, and you like it.

You Trust Them

If you say something to each other and you have no doubt it's true, then you are moving into something more. When one of you says that they love the other person and you know it's true, then you are moving forward.

You Want to Share Your World

There comes a time when you are still independent and have your goals, but you want her to share the journey. You are spending more time together and becoming supportive of each other and cheering victories.

This closeness is the two of you creating a life together. Don't be scared by that. It's natural and is part of any relationship at any stage.

You Feel More Comfortable with Them than Anyone Else

You are still independent, but you feel comfortable with them, and it's like they get you. You support each other and just click.

You Don't Want to Be with Anyone Else

There will come the point where you want to only be with them. You can still appreciate beauty in other women as well as sexiness, but that's all it is. Appreciation.

You no longer have the desire to have sex or even have intimate discussions with other women. You don't want to share anything with anyone else, besides your woman.

Guess what? **You're in love.**

Chapter 10: How to Be Happy in Your Relationship

Being happy in a relationship isn't difficult. There are ups and downs, but as long as you communicate and respect each other, you can have a long happy relationship

Communication

Talking to each other in a relationship is vital.

Tell each other your needs and be open and honest. Don't keep anything from each other. This doesn't mean you need to burden her with everything. Share how you feel, but you don't need to become overly sensitive and tell her every little feeling.

Just be honest, respectful and caring.

Listen

This never changes. You need to listen whenever you are talking with a woman. It doesn't matter if it's the first time you met her or your first date. And this definitely doesn't change when you get into a relationship.

She is going to give you the information you need to keep her happy as well as yourself. If you don't actively listen to her, you'll never know what that information is.

Be Honest

Tell her what you need in the relationship and how you feel. I'm not saying you have to become a fountain of emotion by any means, but she needs to know what you are thinking. She is not a mind reader.

Don't Keep Secrets

Along with being honest, you can't keep secrets if you want to successfully communicate in your relationship. I'm not just talking about with your emotions. Your plans, finances, family problems, these are all things that you shouldn't consciously keep from your partner. That doesn't mean that you should spill it all to her all at once. Rather, don't purposefully hide any of it from her. And if you feel bad about not telling her about something, that probably means that you should.

Be Patient

Communication can be very frustrating. Sometimes, it's hard to put to words exactly what we're thinking and feeling. You need to be patient with your partner and yourself. Otherwise, it'll just be harder to get everything out in a coherent manner.

Pay Attention

Look for signals that something might be wrong, or she might be dealing with something. Keep an eye on body language.

Don't Assume

You know the saying about assuming, right? Well, it's a saying because it's true. When you assume, you make an ass out of you and me.

Ask her what's going on, or what she needs. It's ok to ask for clarification. It doesn't matter if she asked you to fix something around the house or something she's missing from the relationship. Never assume.

Don't Fixate on the Little Things

Don't pick on things. We all have quirks, and if it's something that really bothers you and you can't live with it, maybe you are with the wrong person. But if you constantly pick, it's going to do nothing but push you apart and cause the relationship to disintegrate.

Goals

Planning things together gets you focused on the future and adds to your happiness. It could be short-term like a trip or an event or, if your relationship is further along, something like buying a larger item like a boat or house or even retirement.

This strengthens your bond as a couple and team and lets you both know you are in it for the long haul.

Own Your Feelings

I learned a little trick a long time ago that has helped me immensely. Here it is:

No one else can make you feel anything. You are the one who controls your feelings.

A lot of times we tend to start sentences with "You make me feel-." Sometimes it's positive (You make me feel happy, you make me feel horny...) but often it's negative (You make me feel frustrated/angry/upset). The truth is no one can make you feel anything. Take ownership of your feelings and reaction. Start sentences with "I feel..."

Own Your Mistakes

This is hard for both men and women to do. No one wants to admit when they're wrong or when they've made a mistake, but not owning your mistakes can damage your relationship. The resentment from it will build up over time, and eventually, it'll be too much for an otherwise happy relationship to survive. Remember, you're both human. You'll both make mistakes. When you do, admit it so that you can work past it together and move on.

And if your partner admits that she's wrong, do not say, "I told you so." It's immature, and you'll end up sleeping on the couch for it. And, frankly, I don't know if I'd pity you for it.

Relationship Tests

Depending on where you are in the relationship, she may test you. I talked about conversation tests in *How to Talk to Women*, and many of those apply to relationships as well.

She is always going to test to see if you are listening, so just get used to that. She might also test you on your loyalty. Probably the biggest is going to be honesty.

It might be something that she caught you on or even setting you up to see if you tell the truth, but women tend to constantly test your honesty. It's because honesty connects to so many other things – loyalty, fidelity, and trustworthiness. So, they can tell if you are straying.

The bottom line is be honest and own up to what you have done. If you really care for her, the worst you did is left the milk out. You have a wonderful woman, don't mess it up.

Chapter 11: How to Keep Her Interested and into You

There different things that are going to keep women interested in the early stages versus when you have developed a relationship. Some things are always going to be true, though.

Keep the Relationship Vital

Stay Healthy

Suddenly, you are spending more and more time with someone whom you really like. Maybe you start skipping the gym a few times and eventually just stop going. You might even have moved in together and are enjoying that nesting period.

Then one day you wake up and realize that you've gained over 20 pounds, your clothes don't fit, and your new girl isn't looking at you quite the same.

It's natural to change priorities when you start a relationship. Suddenly, you have something that is fighting for top position in your life. You can't allow your own health and appearance to suffer.

You need to take care of yourself, obviously for your health and wellbeing, but that was also part of what attracted her to you. That drive to be in shape made her want to connect with you. If you lose that you are changing and while she may love the inside, you can't argue against the attraction she's losing.

Part of being a successful man is taking care of your own priorities, and this is one of them, even in a relationship.

Leave Some Mystery in Your Lives

Have you ever talked to an elderly married couple and one of them says something to the effect of I still learn new things about them every day?

Yeah, it's really cute, but it says a lot about the mystery of relationships. You don't need to share every detail with her. Especially in the early days, keep some things back. Make her think what she does and then fill in the blanks later. I talk more about this in *How to Talk To Women*.

There's another area where keeping some mystery in your life can help you. Once you get comfortable with a woman or move in together, barriers come down. Some of these barriers, however, need to stay up.

Close the bathroom door. Just generally try to keep your bodily functions out of sight, smell and hearing.

Communication

Talk to her and not just about the relationship. Keep your conversations interesting and challenging. Use your common interest to spark ideas and debate.

Don't Just Be Together, Do Together

Go out and find some regular things that you can do together that challenge you. Learn new skills, take a class or part in a contest. But do things that challenge you to work together and achieve success as a team.

Travel together and discover new places. Find out where neither of you has ever gone and discover that place together.

Support Her

When you date someone over a longer amount of time, life can happen. They can suffer failures, losses, deaths and general downtime. They are going to need your support.

As guys, we always try to step in and save the situation. It's natural for us, part of the primal protector deep in our caveman's brains.

But in many of these situations, we're going to be powerless to do anything. It's going to be for her to do, for her to work out or grieve, and all you can do is support.

This will deepen your connections to each other and start to create a true bond that can be built upon. It will help remind her why she fell in love with you in the first place.

Keep Your Relationship Active

When you are with someone you like, there's a tendency to just curl up on the couch or bed and never do any of the things you used to enjoy. When this happens, people can get bored and start to doubt their relationship. It's not about the person; it's about having someone to binge TV shows with.

This can be dangerous and cause stagnation in your relationship. One day one of you might sit and ask what they have done with their life. Don't let this happen by making sure you still go out have a life. Make sure she meets your friends and you meet hers. Arrange for date nights and group outings.

Make sure you enjoy discovering the world together and doing things. It will continue to strengthen a lifetime bond.

Cheating

Why Do Women Cheat?

Not Happy Sexually

This doesn't necessarily mean that she's not happy about the amount of sex you are having (although it could be an issue). This could be a situation where she doesn't feel that you pay attention to her needs or doesn't feel that the sex is clicking although they may truly love you.

In a longer-term relationship, it's normal for sexual level to wax and wane. If a woman feels that the "spark" has gone from the relationship, she'll be more likely to give in to external temptation. She might even have already mentally left you and is using this as a real reason to break up. It's a way of making it easier because something real was done. She's trying to force you to break up with her.

It's also possible you are not enough for her. Men always get told they think about nothing but sex, but there are women who, if they don't get enough sex the way they need, they will go elsewhere to fulfill their needs.

Communication Problems

Any time a woman (and a man, for that matter) doesn't feel that their partner is listening to them or really understanding what they are going through, they may turn to another man. There's actually a term for this called an "emotional affair." She may not even be having physical relations with another guy, but she is sharing all her emotions and intimate feelings with him. Those are all the things she used to share with you. Honestly, if she's doing that, then sex with him isn't far behind.

Revenge

Did you cheat on her? Well, she might be trying to even the score.

You might not have even confessed, but she might have found out. She might see it as some sort of game to level the playing field.

It might not even be cheating. Some people can have a warped way of looking at things. You may have lied to her about going out with your friends. To her, it's fair to cheat on you because you did something wrong, too.

My two cents- this is not a healthy relationship, and you might want to especially pay attention to the final chapter of this book.

She's a Girl, Not a Woman

She might be immature and shouldn't have been in the relationship to begin with. If she doesn't understand what it means to be faithful and want to have that in a relationship, then she is going to do things that are wrong and self-destructive.

Unresolved Issues

Maybe she's been cheated on by ex-boyfriends, or perhaps she witnessed one or both of her parents cheat on the other. Maybe something in her past has made her so insecure that she's not ready for a monogamous relationship. No matter what the reason, it's probably best that she works on herself before she enters any serious relationship. It's not fair to either of you.

What Are the Signs She Might Be Cheating on You?

Is she is constantly accusing you of doing things that you aren't? Does she say that you are cheating when it's the furthest thing from your mind?

People tend to accuse other people of things they themselves are doing or thinking of doing. If she is always accusing you of cheating or looking at other women and you don't, there's a chance she might be up to something.

She is trying to take any suspicion off her and create it in you. This way she can deflect any accusations because she is keeping you on the defensive.

She Is Judgmental

Does it feel like she's looking for things that are wrong between the two of you? She might be looking for validation for her actions, or it could be guilt. Either way, out of the ordinary actions are a sign something is up.

Things Are Great

If suddenly everything is amazing, you don't fight and even have great sex but you're not sure how you got to that point, there might be something else going on.

Suddenly, She Looks Really Good

If your woman is suddenly dressing nicer, started going to the gym or wearing new makeup or jewelry, there's a good chance it's not for you.

She Isn't Coming to You for Discussions

If suddenly she isn't talking to you as much or expressing her communication needs, something might be up. It means she's talking to someone and you better hope it's her female friends.

Suddenly Very Protective and Secretive

If she snatches up her phone and won't let you see it or get texts or phone calls they act strangely around, something might be up.

She Accuses You of Cheating

Often, cheaters, both men and women, will project their misdeeds onto their partner to alleviate some of their guilt. If she starts accusing you of cheating out of nowhere, suddenly has problems with you hanging out with your female friends, or becomes paranoid about you being around any women, you might want to start asking her the same questions she's been asking you.

You Just Know

Maybe you aren't having sex anymore. Or she doesn't talk to you. Or the spark is just gone. It doesn't mean she's cheating, but if she's not coming to you with issues, there's a chance she's too engaged with her new lover to care.

Don't go in accusing, but look for concrete lies and evidence.

Chapter 12: When Is It Over?

Relationships are great when they work, but there may come the point where things aren't what they used to be. And you need to make the decision... is it over?

Taking Stock of Your Relationship

If you are beginning to feel that a relationship isn't working for you, you need to take a step back and look at it with a clear head. If you have to, make a list (but I wouldn't suggest showing it to your girlfriend.)

Ask yourself the answers to these questions:

Are Your Needs Being Met?

When a relationship is working, both people feel as though they are being listened to, respected and cared. As it progresses, this can change.

If you feel your needs, whether they are emotional or physical, aren't being met, then something is wrong. You have every right to be happy in a relationship, and if you aren't getting what you need, you need to say something.

Be honest and calm, understanding that she might not have known what you needed. Do you need more time and better communication? Do you need more sex? Do you need more interaction or less? Every relationship is different.

If you have communicated your needs and they still aren't being met, then you need to reexamine where the two of you stand.

Are You Starting to Look Elsewhere?

When something good happens to you, the first person you should want to share it with is your partner in your relationship.

But what if you find you really aren't that excited about sharing and would rather tell another friend, coworker or other females?

This is an obvious sign that things aren't what they once were. Even more than that, you find yourself thinking about sexual fulfillment from other women. Now while it's normal for a guy to look at other women and enjoy it, if you are starting to fantasize and even considering pursuing other relationships, it is time to end the one you are in.

Do Other People Support the Relationship?

Love is blind. If you are totally into someone the world is about them and nothing else matters, including the opinions of family and friends.

But if they have pointed out things like how she treats you or her activities or attitude, it might be good to listen to them with an open mind. If they have no opinions, this speaks volumes as well. How many times have you heard someone talk about what they didn't like about one of your friends' girlfriends after they break up and the guy asks why you didn't tell me?

Here's a trick. Ask your mother what she thinks of your girlfriend. Mothers have an incredible ability to judge women. They are also very good at being honest when you ask them to be.

Are You More Different From Each Other Than You Thought?

After a while, you are going to start learning all about each other. Some things are normal that are different. She might be a vegetarian; she might be politically different or religiously different. These are things that can be worked around. Sometimes.

If they are things that are going to cause major disagreements (or already do), then you need to consider if you have a future. What if you want kids but she doesn't? She might be extremely liberal politically while you are conservative. Is this something the two of you could live with or is it going to lead to constant fighting?

Early on in a relationship or dating, these might not be a big deal, but as you move deeper into the relationship, and are considering if this is for the long haul, they take on a different meaning.

How Often Do You Fight?

Every couple has their disagreements and fights. But if you are fighting a couple of times a week, then something is wrong. If you start staying away from them because you don't want to fight, something is very wrong.

Are You Being Honest with Yourself?

If you have to convince yourself that dating her is the right thing to do, then there is a definite problem. Relationships take work, but you shouldn't have to lie to yourself in order to stay in it.

It might be her behavior and the way she treats you or it might just be that you are lying about your feelings. You might be in different places. She might be in love with you, but you don't see yourself getting to that point with her.

You might have even discussed marriage, and one of you is thinking that's where it's going, but the other doesn't see this. You owe it to her and yourself to be honest.

Does Breaking Up Sound Like A Bad Idea?

If you are thinking things over and start to imagine what life would be like without her, then it's starting to sound like you have already made your decision. If you were truly in love and in a healthy relationship, you would work problems over in your head and figure out ways to fix them so that you are both happy.

But if your mind is wandering to thoughts of freedom, then you really need to consider ending it.

Do You Feel Uncomfortable Being Honest?

If you don't trust your girlfriend, to be honest about your feelings or what is going on in your life, something is definitely wrong.

Once you start keeping things from her, it's a short walk to lying, and at that point, your relationship is officially over.

No Reason to Go Is Not a Reason to Stay

Let's say you've answered the above questions and all of them seem to be normal for a healthy relationship, except for one: does breaking up sound like a bad idea? You stop for a moment, and the more you think about, the more the idea of breaking up appeals to you. It makes you feel freer, and you start imagining everything you would do without her...but then you start to feel guilty. You're not fighting, nobody's cheating, nothing's wrong with the relationship, right? There's no reason to go, so why create all that pain and drama?

I had a friend who was in a relationship for five years. On the outside, they seemed like a perfectly happy couple with no complaints. Then she got an offer to work as an ESL teacher in Brazil, but his job didn't allow him to follow her. From what we were told, he let her go without any problems. Rather than trying to make things work long-distance, they decided to take a break.

The change in my friend was almost instantaneous. He suddenly seemed happier and more relaxed. He was more engaged when we went out, and his laugh was heartier than I had heard in a long time. I hadn't even noticed how different he had been until he had started getting back to his normal self. When I asked him what had happened, he confided in me that he hadn't been happy in his relationship in a long time. He had thought about leaving, but he couldn't find a "good" reason, so he just decided it was better to stay. But he had been miserable, even if he hadn't been showing it to anyone, even his girlfriend. Now that the relationship was finally over with minimal hard feelings, he felt like his old self again.

My friend learned an important lesson the hard way: having no reason to go is not a reason to stay. If you're dissatisfied in a relationship and feel that you would be happier without it, you need to at least talk to your partner about this. You might be able to figure out why you're feeling like this and work on it or realize that it is, indeed, time to move on. You don't want to be like my friend, miserable in a relationship for years just because you can't think of any reason to leave.

How to Break Up

So, how do you do it?

It's never easy. Even when my wife and I divorced, it wasn't easy and we communicated well, and we both knew it was time.

Never Do It Over Text or Email

Not only is this rude and disrespectful, don't think you are going to get away with it. She will tell every one of her friends exactly how you did it, and she won't be kind.

Depending on the situation, you might be able to do it over the phone, but it still won't go as well as you hoped. The best way to do it is in a public place and talk like two adults.

Don't Ghost Her

This is a new phenomenon where people just disappear without an explanation. They don't call, return texts or emails, even dropping and blocking others from social media.

This is a hurtful way to break up and, honestly, I think they should take your man card away if you do it. It's immature and against all the things we have discussed about masculinity.

Take ownership of your decision and be straight with her. It's going to hurt, but it'll be over soon.

Do It at the Right Time

While you don't want to drag it out, be considerate of when you do it. Don't break up with her on a major holiday or her birthday or even after a major loss in her life. Also, don't do it in the morning if she has to go to work. Make sure you do it somewhere without distractions or high profile where people know the two of you.

Don't Wait Until After Sex

Some men will do this thinking it will "soften the blow." Don't. Seriously, don't. It's a sleezy move and will probably get you a stiletto heel flung at your head. Have some class.

Don't Wait Too Long

If you drag it out and allow yourself to become more annoyed or angry with her, you are going to make it ugly. Other things will start to come out, and it could turn into a nasty, drawn-out fight. When you know it's over, end it.

Don't Be Vague

Don't say things like maybe one day you'll work it out, or even that you might think twice. You are making a decision, so be decisive. It's not fair to leave a door open for her if you don't really mean it. Closure is good for her and you.

"We Can Be Friends"

Friendship after a breakup is very difficult, even when you have a shared past and history. If it is meant to be, you can't force it, and it takes time. Even without long history, it took a bit of time before my ex-wife and I were friends, but once we did, it was a good choice.

So now is not the time to suggest it, just concentrate on the break-up, and if you are meant to be friends, it will come later.

Some women also consider the "let's be friends" as trying to keep the door open for sex or "friends with benefits." It's best just to avoid this entanglement and not make her think that's what you are suggesting.

Remember, she is going to relay this entire breakup to her friends, and a version of it will start to get around. You don't want to give her ammunition.

Be Honest

Tell her the truth if she asks. You don't have to be mean or cruel, but you owe her honesty. If you don't feel right in the relationship, tell her. If you have fallen out of love with her, let her know. It's not going to be easy to hear, but she is going to appreciate the honesty much more than some answer that has no real meaning.

And once you have told her, you need to stick to your answer. She might try to negotiate, change your mind, say she can change, but if you have gotten to this point, you know your feelings are real. Let her know that this wasn't something you entered lightly. You care about her no matter what and have put a lot of thought into the decision.

Keep Things to Yourself

Of course, you are going to tell people you broke up, but the details aren't really their business. Be kind, don't talk badly about her, and move on. People will notice, including women you talk to in the future. They'll notice you don't bad mouth your ex, and it'll put you in a better light with them.

Be a Man... Don't Cheat

Part of being a man is being mature and responsible, and mature and responsible men don't cheat. A mature man takes stock of the situation, is honest and takes responsibility and ends the relationship before he starts another one.

Not only are you being a creep (which we have been working on not being for a while) but you are not being fair to yourself. You need to be clear about what you want, and if you are sneaking around behind backs, then it's not possible.

Recovering from the Break-Up

There is some old saying that you need one month of recovery for every year you were in a relationship. I don't know if that's quite true, but it will take you some time depending on how deep and long the relationship was.

Don' let yourself fall into a funk. You might have initially been happy about splitting; you might second-guess your decision or get depressed that you might not find the wrong person. Don't let it get you down.

Don't turn to sex for relief. Don't go on some sort of sexual bender on Tinder. Be smart. Also, don't turn to drinking if you are hurting.

Remember to take care of yourself during this time. It will be tempting to turn to any number of addicting behaviors, including drugs and overeating, as well as falling back on bad habits or rebounding to old girlfriends. You might even slip into a bout of depression and let certain parts of your everyday routine fall through the cracks. Do your best to keep up your self-care. It'll help you feel better more quickly.

Just give yourself some time to rest before you head back out there. You'll know how much time you need.

You might decide that you want to try again with her, and sometimes that works. Just make sure you are doing it for the right reasons. Go through your list again and remember why you spilled. If you truly think you were wrong, go over the list again. If you still think you were wrong, maybe give her a call.

No matter what, you will find love again because you know how to be attractive to women.

One Last Reminder Before Conclusion

Have you grabbed your free resource?

A lot of information has been covered in this book. As previously shared, I've created a simple mind map that you can use *right away* to easily understand, quickly recall and readily use what you've learned in this book.

If you've not grabbed it...

Click Here To Get Your Free Resource

Alternatively, here's the link:

https://viebooks.club/freeresourcemind-mapforhowtoattractwomen

Your Free Resource Is Waiting..

Get Your Free Resource Now!

Conclusion

So, how do you feel? Do you see how you can change your life and be attractive to women?

It isn't a crazy secret or about putting up a false front. It's really just about confidence, being genuine and honestly observing and listening to what is around you.

When I discovered all of this, it changed my life, and it has meant the world to me to be able to share it with you. I know that you will now have better experiences with women and a happier, more fulfilled life. That is a great feeling to share with you.

Use this book as a guide whenever you need it to keep moving forward with your growth in interacting with women. Come back to it to answer questions or when you need help with specific problems.

I would urge you to also pick up ***How to Flirt with Women*** and ***How to Talk to Women*** if you haven't already. In those books, I delve into specifics on how to flirt and have conversations, great ways to start conversations, and how to pick up on signs. Also, delve deeper into presentation and other aspects of dating.

Always remember to keep the right mindset and be confident.

Good luck out there, guys.

Sincerely,

Ray Asher

P.S.

If you've found this book helpful in any way, a review on Amazon is greatly appreciated.

This means a lot to me, and I'll be extremely grateful.

Notes

[1] Thomas M. M. Versluys and William J. Skylark. "The effect of leg-to-body ratio on male attractiveness depends on the ecological validity of the figures." *The Royal Society* (2017)

[2] Reed, J. Ann and Blunk, Elizabeth. "The influence of facial hair on impression formation." *Social Behavior and Personality: An International Journal. Volume 18, Number 1* (1990): 169-175.

More Books By Ray Asher

How to Flirt with Women: The Art of Flirting Without Being Creepy That Turns Her On! How to Approach, Talk to & Attract Women (Dating Advice for Men)

How To Flirt With Any Woman Successfully – <u>The Ultimate Guide</u>

Are you unhappy with your dating life?

Are you craving female attention and sex, but not getting them?

Do you secretly feel unattractive because of some rejections you've faced in the past?

If you want to stop all these in your life, then keep reading...

Research shows that most women – even those who appear tough – are secretly looking for romance.

But no matter how you look like, how much money you have, or how muscular your body is...if you don't know **how to <u>flirt</u> with women**, you'll appear as:

- Needy

- Desperate

- Boring

- Lacking social intelligence

- Simply ...unattractive.

Flirting is the art of small talk. It includes a lot of playfulness, smooth conversation skills, and high social intelligence. In fact, with the right words, right tonality, and right "approach" – you can make ANY woman highly attracted to you.

In this book, **Ray Asher will show you how to flirt like a pro**.

Ray Asher used to be an introverted teenager who didn't have the courage to approach girls. He started dating a girl he liked in college – only to find she was cheating on him regularly. His pain drove him to go out every night and day, speak with women, and discover what makes them attracted. After thousands of rejections, a few "friends with benefits" and lots of notes – he discovered the power of flirting, and decided to share his knowledge with any men who wishes to become good with women.

This book is the most comprehensive guide ever written about flirting.

Here's a taste of what you'll discover inside *How to Flirt with Women*:

- Exactly what to say to make a conversation flirty and amusing

- Tonality tricks that make you look confident, funny and charismatic

- Four crucial principles of flirting that work for all women of all cultures

- How to create a "leader" frame in every conversation you have with women, and make them respect you

- The EXACT words and gestures that impress women

- How to text a girl and how to flirt online (with detailed tips for every social network)

- Techniques on how to approach and talk to women in different places and different social situations (at work, while traveling, at restaurants, farmers' markets – you name it!)

And much, much more...

Q: "But how can I be sure this book will work FOR ME?"

The dating advice for men in this book was written from experience, and was proven to work for people all over the world. Flirting is simply a way to transfer sexual emotions, it can work in any language with any woman. Readers who have tried the information in this book were SHOCKED to see how effective it is, even those virgins and those who never approached a woman before. If they can do it – SO CAN YOU!

Just buy the book, read the information and EX-ECUTE!

If you're ready to finally learn the art of flirting with women and become an attractive guy, now is the time.

How to Talk to Women: Get Her to Like You & Want You With Effortless, Fun Conversation & Never Run Out of Anything to Say! How to Approach Women (Dating Advice for Men)

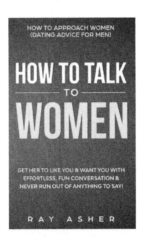

Discover How to Master the Art of Conversation, Effortlessly Engage and Deeply Connect with Women and Dramatically Improve Your Dating Life!

Tired of freezing up when in close proximity to an attractive woman you'd like to talk to?

Do you often run out of things to say when talking with a woman, only to watch her slowly lose interest?

If you want to stop all these in your life, then keep reading...

Learning how to effortlessly talk to women and getting them to open up to you is a skill that so few men have and can open up a world that you never knew existed.

Women are more likely to do you favors and even date you if you know how to approach and properly connect with them.

And it doesn't have to be difficult.

In this powerful guide, Ray Asher condenses his years of struggles, trials and errors and his eventual discovery of the secrets of deeply connecting with and attracting women using the power of conversation to help you bring the kind of women you desire into your life.

***How to Talk to Women*, the only book you'll ever need to connect with women on a level she'd never experienced before.**

Here's a taste of what you'll discover inside *How to Talk to Women*:

- The 4 surefire conversational topics that are universally engaging to women

- 5 foolproof ways to have memorable conversations with women

- Simple tips to help you avoid turning off a woman with "mansplaining"

- An effective conversational template that you never run out of things to say

- 10 powerful listening tips to make a woman feel completely understood by you

- Effortless ways to get her to discuss sexual topics with you

- How to get past the small talk and get into a deep conversation with a woman

- 6 topics to avoid like the plague when in a conversation with a woman you're interested in

- How to tell an insanely good story that will have her hanging onto your every word

- Dating advice for men and pro tips to help you smoothly ask for her digits

And much, much more...

Whether you're completely clueless when it comes to women, or you're looking to sharpen your conversational skills with them, this guide will get you started on the way to a more charming, attractive version of yourself.

If you're ready to finally learn how to effortlessly talk to women without breaking a sweat, attract them and say goodbye to overwhelming shyness, now is the time.

Printed in Great Britain
by Amazon

40133558R00116